REVIEW COPY

A Selection of Hebrew Melodies, Ancient and Modern, by Isaac Nathan and Lord Byron

Portrait of Isaac Nathan.
(Courtesy of Charles Venour Nathan)

A Selection of Hebrew Melodies, Ancient and Modern, by Isaac Nathan and Lord Byron

Edited, with Introduction and Notes,
by Frederick Burwick
and Paul Douglass

Published by
The University of Alabama Press
Tuscaloosa and London

Copyright © 1988 by
The University of Alabama Press
Tuscaloosa, Alabama 35487
All rights reserved
Manufactured in the United States of America

Publication of this book has been assisted
by a grant from the Publications Program of the
National Endowment for the Humanities

LIBRARY OF CONGRESS CATALOGING-IN-PUBLICATION DATA

Nathan, Isaac, 1792–1864.
  A selection of Hebrew melodies, ancient and modern.

  For 1–3 voices with piano and 4 voices.
  Reprint. Originally published: London: I. Nathan,
1815–1816.
  Words printed as text with each song.
  Includes index.
  Bibliography: p.
  1. Songs with piano. 2. Vocal quartets,
Unaccompanied. 3. Vocal duets with piano. 4. Vocal
trios with piano. 5. Byron, George Gordon Byron,
Baron, 1788–1824—Musical settings. I. Byron,
George Gordon Byron, Baron, 1788–1824. II. Burwick,
Frederick. III. Douglass, Paul, 1951–   .
IV. Title. V. Title: Hebrew melodies.
M3.1.N37S4 1988   87-750758
ISBN 0-8173-0373-1 (alk. paper)

British Library Cataloguing-in-Publication Data is available.

To

Charles Venour Nathan
of New South Wales,
great-great-grandson of the composer

Contents

List of Illustrations   viii

Acknowledgments   ix

Introduction: The Creation of "Hebrew" Melodies   1

Notes to the Introduction   37

About Performance   40

About the Texts   41

A Selection of Hebrew Melodies, Ancient and Modern, by Isaac Nathan and Lord Byron

Songs of 1815–1816   45

Additional Songs   191

Notes on the Songs   240

Bibliography   243

Index   245

Illustrations

Isaac Nathan *frontispiece*

Lord Byron in Albanian Costume   3

John Braham, by Robert Dighton   5

"The Jew & the Gentile"   6

"Fare Thee Well," by George Cruikshank   9

"Jephtha's Daughter"   20

Acknowledgments

The facsimile of *A Selection of Hebrew Melodies, Ancient and Modern* (1815–1816) has been photographically reproduced from the copy held in the private collection of Mr. and Mrs. Jack Gumpert Wasserman. The editors wish to thank Mr. and Mrs. Wasserman for permission to reproduce this exceptionally well-preserved copy, autographed on the title page by Isaac Nathan and John Braham.

The reproduction of the additional songs from the 1824–1829 edition of *Hebrew Melodies,* and of "Bright Be the Place of thy Soul" (sheet music) is by gracious permission of the Mitchell Library, State Library of New South Wales, Sydney, Australia. The editors are most grateful for the help of Martin Beckett, Baiba Berzins, and the staff of the library.

The works of Isaac Nathan, with a catalogue of 136 musical compositions, as well as family records before and after Nathan's immigration to Australia, are contained in the private collection of Charles Venour Nathan, great-great-grandson of the composer, who resides in Vaucluse, New South Wales. Mr. Nathan, to whom this volume is dedicated, provided invaluable assistance to the editors. He made courteous responses to their inquiries, willingly consulted family records in order to document biographical details, and corrected several inadvertent errors.

The editors also gratefully acknowledge the permission of the British Museum and the National Portrait Gallery to reproduce illustrations in the text of the introduction.

Introduction: The Creation of "Hebrew" Melodies

BYRON'S *Hebrew Melodies* have so long been considered neither authentically "Hebrew" nor particularly "melodic" that it will come as a surprise to many that they are genuinely both. Byron's pose of Jewishness was not antic but studied. While it outraged a number of reviewers, others, including the Jewish poet Heinrich Heine, applauded the bold performance. More importantly, however, the poems are truly "lyric": Byron wrote all but a few of them in close collaboration with the young Jewish composer Isaac Nathan. Nathan gathered tunes in London and Canterbury synagogues and arranged them in give-and-take with Byron, who wrote poems in response to the music. Published on the eve of Byron's scandalous and permanent departure from England, the *Melodies* sold well. They were reissued in an expanded version following Byron's death in 1824. Through the succeeding generation, the *Melodies* lingered as sheaves upon the parlor piano. Gradually, the once-popular work was forgotten. Thus a rather remarkable moment in Byron's career, in the "national airs" period of musical history, and in the history of English Jews, lapsed into obscurity.

This facsimile edition, which includes the entire contents of the original *Hebrew Melodies* of 1815–1816 together with additional songs published later,[1] will make Nathan's music available again and enable us to reconsider it and Byron's lyrics in the light of their two-year collaboration. For students of Byron's work, this replication of the true first edition of such lyrics as "She Walks in Beauty" and "Jephtha's Daughter" will make it possible to appraise the poems in their original context. Inevitably, it will change the way we *hear* the poems. For scholars of music, the collection will restore part of the record of a developing English popular song and Romantic art-music.

Nathan tried a little of everything in arranging his tunes,

Portrait of Lord Byron in Albanian Costume. During his first tour abroad, begun in July 1809, Byron and John Cam Hobhouse visited Jannina in Albania and were fitted with costumes. In the spring of 1814, Byron sat for Thomas Phillips' portrait. The costume is in the Museum of Costume at the Assembly Rooms, Bath, England.
(National Portrait Gallery, London)

both succeeding, as in "We sate down and wept," and failing, as in his maudlin setting of "Thy Days are Done." What is fascinating about the *Hebrew Melodies* as a whole is that they constitute a crossroads of contemporary musical fashion. The tastes of English listeners in the middle of the Regency period were vastly different from those which would prevail a scant five years later, when the performances of Paganini in Milan had made him synonymous with Romanticism, when Liszt had finally made his debut at the tender age of nine, and when "Gretchen am Spinnrade" and "Der Erlkönig" would be published as Schubert's Opus 1 and 2. Indeed, we forget too easily that the German high style achieved a genuine vogue only around 1830, and a centrality in concert repertoire some twenty years after that. There was as yet no clear dividing line between art and popular song, and the former tended to look for its models to Haydn, whose canzonets had achieved quite a popularity during his visit to London in the 1790s.

When late-Victorian and Edwardian critics surveyed the *Hebrew Melodies,* they were not well disposed toward its eclectic and ornamented style. Their opinions about Nathan's work contributed to an obscurity that has deepened with time, so that Byron's poetry, its connection to the original musical project essentially lost, stood alone. Although Thomas L. Ashton documented the facts of the collaboration in his variorum edition (1972), he could offer no informed appraisal of the music, nor of how that music might be evident in Byron's lyrics.[2] In editing the *Hebrew Melodies* for *The Complete Poetical Works* (vol. III, 1983), Jerome J. McGann quite rightly turned to Ashton in his collation of the text; and in his commentary on the poems, he could find no more helpful account of the musical settings.[3] No verdict on the *Hebrew Melodies* has yet been formed that is based on a full dossier of the case. As recently as 1979, the Royal Musical Association's *Musica Britannica* volume of *English Songs: 1800-1860* erroneously attributed the arrangements to John Braham, describing Nathan as simply "a London Jew."[4]

To help correct such errors, and to afford the reader and performer with an adequate background to the music, we have set for ourselves four tasks in this introductory essay: First, to recount briefly the story of Nathan's project. Second, to describe what is known of the music's Hebrew sources. Third, to evaluate how Byron put on "Jewishness" in his lyrics. And fourth, to make a tentative assessment of the character and quality of the music.

Nathan's
Hebrew Melodies

The son of *chazan* (cantor) Menehem Mona, Isaac Nathan (1790?–1864) was born into a time of major, yet frustrating and problematic, change for English Jews. While England was, in comparison with the Continent, an island of toleration, it was still no haven from anti-Semitism. True, Canterbury afforded Nathan many opportunities not available to Jews born in, say, Frankfurt or Warsaw. Nevertheless, his ambition to achieve professional recognition and financial security were baffled by a social system that excluded Jews.

Through his father's hard work and careful planning, Nathan was among the fortunate few who came to attend the first Jewish boarding school at Cambridge. The headmaster, Solomon Lyon, directed Nathan's preparation for the rabbinate and arranged his attendance at the University, where Jews were debarred from taking a degree. By the time he completed his studies in 1808, he had decided on a career in music. Reluctantly, his father allowed him to pursue that course, and in 1810 he apprenticed his son to Domenico Corri (1746–1825), one of the premier singing masters, music publishers, and concert promoters in London.

This alteration in the son's plans must have cost his father a great deal, in both money and disappointment. But Nathan had convinced him that opportunities for Jews were expanding, particularly on the stage. Corri, the former pupil of one of opera's truly legendary teachers, Nicolo Porpora (1686–1767), published in 1810 a book on vocal training, *The Singer's Preceptor,* which was doing well. Corri's activity as a music publisher stretched back thirty years to his edition, one of the earliest, of national airs, *A Select Collection of Forty Scotch Songs* (1780), and suggested to Nathan a career combining such publication with voice and keyboard instruction adjoined to a career on the stage itself. In this, he sought to emulate not only his master, but also his master's associate, John Braham (1777?–1856), the first *chazan* to move successfully into a career of singing on the stage and composing songs for the theater.[5]

Jews certainly were succeeding as artists and musicians in the early years of the nineteenth century, and they were even gaining acceptance in scientific and philosophical societies with distinguished memberships including men like Thomas Babington Macaulay and Samuel Taylor Coleridge. But as Todd Endelman points out, professing Jews remained unwelcome in fashionable society even later in the Victorian period.[6] Political emancipation of the Jew began to bring results when the freedom to carry on retail trade was extended to Jews in 1831, when the Christian Oath of Abjuration was abolished in 1835, and when the measure admitting Jews to Parliament passed in 1858. Legally, English Jews held a paradoxical position: not yet enfranchised, their votes were nevertheless tallied. Yet when they insisted on their rights, they were rebuffed. One illustration of this is the famous Bedford Charity case of 1816, which occurred even as Nathan was enjoying the popular success of *Hebrew Melodies*.

The Bedford Charity maintained a free school; it paid for and rewarded the completion of apprenticeships, and granted marriage portions to poor girls. Sheba Lyon's father

Introduction / 4

had lived in the town for two decades, and had actually voted regularly in the annual elections for trustees of the charity. Yet she was denied the right to draw for an apprentice fee. The trustees feared that the charity's liberality had attracted too many Jews to Bedford. The Lyon family sued, with the help of the influential Goldsmid brothers. They lost.[7] This case reminded English Jews that their rights depended on the good will of the gentile majority. During the war with France, that good will was undermined by a resurgent xenophobia. Jews found themselves the victims of the Aliens Act of 1793, and as late as 1813 the Birmingham Synagogue was attacked by a mob. Under the mandate of the Mendelssohnian movement, Jews were encouraged to look beyond the ghetto. But accommodation and assimilation most often meant that they must disguise or deny their heritage.

Thus, in a period when they were becoming, practically speaking, "enfranchised," English Jews actively de-emphasized and often renounced their own Jewishness. During the Anglo-French war, Jews entered military service in unprecedented numbers. Their political loyalties, as Geoffrey Alderman has noted, conformed to the dominant trends: During the mid-eighteenth century they were Whigs; by 1800, they supported the younger Pitt.[8] They elected political leaders, yet not one—not Menassah Lopes, nor Ralph Franco, nor Ralph Bernal, nor David Ricardo—was actually a professing Jew. The Christian Oath of Abjuration, after all, made it technically impossible for a professing Jew to hold office. Even after the oath was abolished, Jews still found it difficult to pursue a political career. While Isaac D'Israeli never renounced his faith, he quarreled with the officials of the synagogue in Bevis Marks and had his children baptized—including young Benjamin, whose christening in 1817 made possible his ensuing political career. At all levels in the Jewish world, the ambitious were compelled to the baptismal font.

Portrait of John Braham, by Robert Dighton.
(National Portrait Gallery, London)

Introduction / 5

"The Jew & the Gentile," an 1803 cartoon by Rowlandson. Charles Incledon, caricatured on the left, was a rival of John Braham, at right. This drawing was occasioned by Braham's successful appearance in *Family Quarrels*. The invidious comparisons suggested are in physiognomy and musical style: note that Braham's absurd cadenza is followed by a trill said to "shake" for seventeen minutes, while Incledon, by contrast, sings in the sweet, simple, Italian mode.

An account of another such defection may help to illustrate in what ways Nathan's story typifies his time. Francis Palgrave (1788–1861) was born Francis Cohen, the son of a wealthy stockbroker. Like Nathan, he acquired a taste for a life not available in the Jewish community, a taste that was nourished by the education his father provided for him. Cohen began to seek intellectual companionship outside his ethnic community, for even among the Anglo-Jewish elite, an education such as the one he and Isaac Nathan had received was unusual. Cohen got himself baptized, then married and changed his name. He went on to a stellar career at the bar, was knighted in 1832, and became keeper of public records. Like other ambitious Jews of the period, he had in effect abandoned his heritage. In 1816, John Braham himself married a Miss Bolton, who would bear him six children—all of whom would be raised in the Church of England.[9]

Nathan also married, in 1812, a gentile named Elizabeth Rosetta Worthington, a seventeen-year-old girl who had been one of his pupils. But his marriage and career turned out differently from those of Palgrave and Braham. Nathan neither changed his name nor renounced his Judaism. Instead, his wife is recorded in the synagogue documents as a convert to the Jewish faith. Such conversions, while not uncommon in lower-class families, were highly unusual for one of Miss Worthington's social station. She had given up her family and friends by marrying her handsome young singing master.[10] For Nathan's part, his marriage did nothing to remove the barrier between him and the musicians, composers, playwrights, and performers whose company he longed to join at Covent Garden, Drury Lane, and Vauxhall Gardens. Although the English middle and upper classes tolerated Jews, they wanted them to keep their place.

In the *London Magazine* (August 1821), Charles Lamb objects to "the approximation of the Jew and Christian which has become so fashionable. . . . Jews christianizing—Christians judaising—puzzles me." Consequences of this "confounding piece of anomaly" Lamb observes in the performances of John Braham, who should have "abided by the faith of his forefathers." Braham is a fine singer, Lamb argues, only because he conquers his Christian pretensions when he sings. Braham's rendition of "And the children of Israel went on dry land through the sea" (from Handel's *Israel in Egypt*) powerfully reveals how "the Hebrew spirit is strong in him, in spite of his proselytism." Admiration combines with fear in Lamb's praise, "The auditors, for the moment, are as Egyptians to him, and he rides over our necks in triumph." And he frankly confesses, "I have not the nerves to enter their synagogues. Old prejudices cling about me."[11]

Lamb's statements reveal the stubborn character of prejudice among Englishmen otherwise disposed, as Byron was, toward generosity of spirit and openhandedness in behavior. The message for unconverted Jews was simple: Thus far, but no farther. Former Jews might become MPs, actual Jews might help win the war with France (as the Goldsmids and Rothschilds had done), and a Jew might even be elected sheriff (David Salomons in 1835), but the image of the Jew remained essentially unchanged through the first decades of the nineteenth century. As late as 1834, *The Universal Songster* included fifty "Jews' Songs," the comic protagonists of which were lenders and vendors. In truth, Jewish peddlers and shopkeepers in London numbered in the thousands during the Regency period, and their caftans, large broad-brimmed hats, and street cries left an indelible impression on all observers. No doubt that impression was deeply felt by John Braham and Francis Palgrave. Isaac Nathan, however, chose neither to remain within the fold of his community nor to abandon it to enter the gentile world.

Admittedly, other factors contributed to the rough ups and downs of Nathan's career. His dream to follow Braham onto the stage was never to be fulfilled. He had a good voice, but, as William Hazlitt wrote of his debut in the musical production of *Guy Mannering* at Covent Garden (February 1820), he lacked "the capacity of sending out a sufficient volume of articulate sound to fill a large theatre." The part of Bertram, which Braham had played at Drury Lane (October 1819), Nathan performed so poorly that Hazlitt judged "neither . . . his manner of speaking, nor his action, at all fitted for the stage."[12] He tried as late as the 1830s to assert himself as a theater tenor, but never succeeded. He had considerable talent as a composer and wrote some excellent individual pieces—"Why are you wandering here, I pray?" for example, from James Kenney's *Sweethearts and Wives* (1823), was the most popular song in London in its day. Francis Cohen, a detractor of *Hebrew Melodies,* has said that this song showed Nathan's great potential, that it "almost attained the dignity of a national song, and a new edition was called for as late as 1883."[13] Following the success of *Sweethearts and Wives,* Nathan also provided scores for Kenney's *The Alcaid* (1824) and *The Illustrious Stranger* (1827), and his songs were as popular as any among the ephemera of theater music. He was engaged to compose and perform concerts in Vauxhall Gardens and for the private entertainments of Lady Caroline Lamb.[14] Like Corri, he was an excellent singing master, and like Corri, he published a widely respected book on vocal technique, *Musurgia Vocalis* (1823).[15] He was George IV's music librarian, and he taught voice to Princess Charlotte of Wales, to whom *Hebrew Melodies* is dedicated. Despite friends in court, he was never secure. At the close of the decade, he performed some espionage for William IV. When Victoria came to the throne in 1837, this service was not honored; he was dismissed, unpaid, with over £2,000 debt incurred. His entreaties availing nothing, he was forced to emigrate to Australia in 1840. There he distinguished himself as the "Father of Australian Music." In 1864 he was killed, stepping from a tram on a street in Sydney. He left behind him a remarkable record of publication and promotion of music—and a family that proliferated into composition and performance. His grandson is even a claimant to the authorship of "Waltzing Matilda."[16]

Of all his music, Nathan was proudest of *Hebrew Melodies*—and with reason. Though the music, like its maker, has traveled a rocky road and fallen into neglect, it remains a considerable achievement. Nathan had genuine ability, and he lavished care on this project with the consciousness that it would, if successful, make his career, establishing him in the highly lucrative but crowded "national melodies" market, which already included such works as: *Select Collection of Original Scottish Airs* (1793, 1804), *A Selection of Irish Melodies* (1808), *A Selection of Scottish Melodies* (1812), and *Select Collection of Original Irish Airs* (1814). That market had been created by George Thomson, Sir John Stevenson, Thomas Moore, Henry R. Bishop, and Horace Twiss. It even included collections of Indian and Welsh songs brought out by the prodigious publishing house of James Power in Dublin. Thomson himself had tried to interest Byron in a National Melodies project just before Nathan came up with his own entry, but the poet had turned down the idea, not wishing to embarrass himself by trying to rival his friend, Thomas Moore. "It is not a species of writing which I undervalue," Byron wrote to Thomson, adding that he had no desire to compete with Burns and Moore, "men whom it were difficult to imitate and impossible to equal."[17]

Nathan intended to capitalize on the current literary fashion for the stereotypical "wildness and pathos" of Jews, and placed an advertisement in the May 1813 issue of *Gentleman's Magazine,* announcing that he was about to publish a book of "Hebrew Melodies," "all of them upwards of 1000 years old and some of them performed by the Antient Hebrews before the destruction of the temple." Such striking claims would certainly attract attention. Nathan appears to have sincerely assumed the endurance of traditional melodies, although his belief in their antiquity ("upwards of 1000 years old," indeed!) was raw even in a time of small musicological sophistication. He had no lyricist, and may not yet have gathered much music among the synagogues of the German Jews in Canterbury and London. He had supposed, rightly as it turned out, that the German traditions were better preserved.

Around him, he saw many composers catering to the lower levels of taste. The leading composer of musical drama from this time into the mid–1830s was Henry Bishop (1786–1855), who frequently joined with the prolific Dibdin family to produce opera and popular songs. Charles Dibdin and his sons wrote hundreds of ballads and songs in the first decades of the century, collaborating with Bishop, Reeve, Attwood (who also wrote for Thomas Moore), Moorehead, Kelly, and Sanderson. Plainly, while European composers were creating some of the most ambitious and influential pieces of music history, England failed to develop much serious art music. Economic prosperity seems to have contributed to the fact that, as Leon

Introduction / 7

Plantinga has said, England was in the early 1800s a dull place for artists.[18] To attempt something more creative and ambitious, Nathan would not settle for a hack rhymester. He went looking for a true poet. He wrote Sir Walter Scott in the winter of 1813–1814, but he was turned down. Then he sent Lord Byron a setting for some lines from the *Bride of Abydos* ("This rose," Canto I, 287–326). Not long after, on 30 June 1814, he wrote a long letter asking—begging, almost—to play some melodies for Byron.[19] Nathan had gone ahead to set some lines from *Lara* ("Night wanes," Canto II, 1–18). He had also appealed to Braham and to Douglas Kinnaird, who were associated with Byron at the Drury Lane Theatre. On September 15, Kinnaird wrote to Byron: "if you would give him a few lines (if only for one air) the sale of his work would be Secur'd & his pocket enrich'd."

At this point, Kinnaird was still repeating Nathan's claim that the music was identical with that sung by the Jews "ere our blessed Lord & Saviour came into the world to be the cause of the persecution of these bearded men." Kinnaird vouched for Nathan's ability to write beautiful settings. In the meantime, Braham had tentatively agreed to assist, and to perform the songs at Drury Lane. Byron acquiesced, sending Nathan a small sheaf of poems that apparently included "She Walks in Beauty," "Sun of the Sleepless," "Francisca," and "It is the Hour," as well as one that may have been written impromptu for the occasion, "Oh! Weep for those." Nathan was in business, and Kinnaird wrote Byron on 19 September 1814 with thanks: "The benefit conferr'd on my protégé is really an important one. . . . It is a great satisfaction to me to be able to assure you that your kindness & Poetry will be conferr'd on both worth & talent."[20]

There is every reason to suppose Nathan thought that would be the end of his "collaboration" with Byron. He had his poems and could use the poet's name. He would not have expected that Byron could write lyrics sympathetic to Jewish culture and history, nor that, if he could, he would want to—and judging from Nathan's choice of Scott, that was no objection anyway. Nathan certainly knew what was popular and what was likely to sell in the London of 1814. Educated taste had been shaped massively by Purcell and Handel. Popular taste had been molded by the meretricious trilling of the stage on which the Dibdins', Arnold's, and Kenney's words had been sung to the music of King and Braham and others—what Leigh Hunt accurately labeled "catchpenny lyrics."[21] And everyone had been impressed by the excesses of Braham, who had a voice of unparalleled power, range, and flexibility, but who (according to Rimbault) liked to dazzle the gallery and "continued to introduce long cadenzas and florid passages when such things had fallen out of fashion." Arranging the melodies would be a tricky business indeed. Nathan would have to achieve a stylishly "Antient" Jewishness (with the quotation marks intact). At the same time, he would have to cater to Braham's audience (the singer's name would appear on *Hebrew Melodies*) and to the taste of those like Kinnaird, who liked the setting Nathan had done of the lines from *Lara* because "the music is in Handel's style."

But the exchange between Byron and Nathan ripened unexpectedly into a true joint venture. Nathan set the poems he had been given and brought them to Byron, along with other tunes he had transcribed. Pleased, and perhaps even astonished to hear "She Walks in Beauty" transformed into an Invocation of the Muse, and "Sun of the Sleepless!" changed (by the cantorial melodic line repeating the phrase "powerless rays") from the complaint of an unrequited Petrarchan lover into a lamentation of the exiled and estranged, Byron again struck off more lines. "At the time his Lordship was writing for me the poetry to these melodies," Nathan later said, "he felt anxious to facilitate my views in preserving as much as possible the original airs, for which purpose he would frequently consult me regarding the style and metre of his stanzas. I accordingly desired to be favoured with so many lines, some pathetic, some playful, others martial, &c."[22] At the end of their first month of collaboration, Byron wrote to Annabella Milbanke that he had found Nathan's music "beautiful," and laughed that "this should fall to my lot, who have been abused as 'an infidel.' Augusta says 'they will call me a *Jew* next'."[23] The collaboration grew spontaneously and rapidly. By 24 December 1814, when the poet set off to Seaham for his marriage to Annabella, Byron and Nathan had preliminary arrangements for seventeen songs. In January and February, the first two months after the wedding, Annabella transcribed another eleven lyrics for the collection. Nathan, however, waited until after Byron had returned to London and settled in Piccadilly Terrace, so that he could share his arrangements with Byron and alter the settings to suit the poet. One morning in June, 1815, Byron provided Nathan with the twenty-ninth and last song, "Bright be the place of thy soul," which the composer promptly set and performed that evening at Byron's request for Drury Lane's beloved Falstaff, William Dowton. The following spring, when Nathan was working out the finishing touches just prior to Byron's departure, there was still opportunity for him to test the poet's response to the music.

Leigh Hunt recounts hearing Nathan perform during such a session with Byron, when "the noble Bard, who was then in the middle of that unpleasant business about his wife, asked him for one respecting Herod and Mariamne, which he listened to with an air of romantic regret." Hunt quietly savors the macabre irony of Byron indulging "romantic regret" over Herod's executing his beloved, and he expressly delights in Nathan's dramatic rendition: "Mr. Nathan had a fine head; and made the grand pianoforte shake like a nut shell under the vehemence of his inspiration."[24] In spite of the scandal and the confusion attending his departure from England, the poet took the time to bid his composer a cordial farewell. Byron gave Nathan a £50 note (an extravagance he could not well afford at the time) and thanked him for his parting gift (it was Passover) of matzos (to Nathan, 16 or 23 April 1816).

Thus Nathan, who had been hoping for a song or two, ended with twenty-nine, more than he could include in the first edition of *Hebrew Melodies*. Unfortunately, Byron's publisher, John Murray, also wanted the *Hebrew Melodies* for a complete edition of Byron's poetry. Byron wrote Nathan an apologetic letter, explaining Murray's wish and asking Nathan to "allow him that privilege without considering it an infringement on your copyright," but granting that "it is against all good fashion to give and take back" (January 1815). Nathan, who had expected exclusive rights, had no desire to share the poems. But Byron had already written Murray that Kinnaird would "have the goodness to furnish copies of the Melodies" (6 January 1815). By the end of the month, he realized and regretted his mistake: "'The Melodies',—damn the melodies, I have other tunes—or rather tones—to think of; but Murray *can't* have them, or *shan't*, or I shall have Kin^d [Kinnaird] and Braham upon me" (To Hobhouse, 26 January 1815). Accepting Hobhouse's determination "that it is not precisely the same thing to have music made to one's poems, and to write poetry for music,"[25] Murray proceeded with an edition of the poems, and Nathan hastened to prepare the publication of the melodies so his collaboration with Byron would not be obscured and discredited. From the seventeen lyrics Nathan had already received before Byron left London in December, Nathan assembled his first sequence of twelve songs. These he managed to see through the press by April 1815, a full month before Murray brought out the poems. Losing no time, Nathan continued rehearsing the new melodies with Byron. A year later, on 18 April 1816, he was ready with his second volume, which appeared with a new issue of the first volume, each containing a set of twelve songs. The scandal accompanying Byron's departure from England provided an unanticipated surge of sales. Despite the unwanted competition with Murray, Nathan's project achieved initial success, though, as we know, Murray's musicless "melodies" eventually eclipsed the original.

When Nathan recollects this period of collaboration in the notes to his second edition of *Hebrew Melodies* (in four

"Fare Thee Well," by George Cruikshank, 1816. In this cartoon, Byron holds the actress, Mrs. Mardyn, and waves to Lady Byron, who stands on shore holding infant daughter Ada. Other women in the boat with Byron are additional actresses from Drury Lane Theatre. "I say, Jack," notes one of the shipboard observers. "I hopes he's got enough of 'em aboard!" (Courtesy of Trustees of the British Museum)

Introduction / 9

numbers, 1824–1829) and in his *Fugitive Pieces* (1829), he may be guilty of an overfond exaggeration of the friendship he felt Byron reciprocated, but he cannot be charged with fabricating the account of the composition of individual songs. Since Nathan's *Fugitive Pieces* is in many instances the only source for insight into the collaboration, it is important to examine the reliability of his "reminiscences." Where other records exist, they tally well with the *Fugitive Pieces*.

For example, Nathan claims that when the first volume of *Hebrew Melodies* appeared in April 1815, Scott (not yet Sir Walter) came twice to visit him at his home in Poland Street, once in company with his wife and daughter, to hear Nathan perform. As unlikely as it may seem, Scott did indeed make an excursion, with Mrs. Scott and his daughter Sophia, from Edinburgh to London (March 31 to June 11, 1815) and recorded his concern to introduce Sophia to music and the arts. In a letter eight months later (22 November 1815), Nathan reminds Scott of the visit and tries to interest him in contributing lyrics to a collection "on the same plan as the Hebrew Melodies."[26] Such evidence may be tangential, but it supports Nathan's credibility. Consider again Leigh Hunt's account of his visiting Byron on the eve of his departure from England. Hunt corroborates, even on the songs Nathan sang for Byron, the scene recalled in *Fugitive Pieces*.[27] Although he tends to render Byron's conversation with little more skill than that of an amateur court scribe, Nathan manages to capture sufficient authenticity to convince us that he kept thorough notes. Byron's three letters to Nathan reveal a polite social responsiveness, and Nathan uses them (with holographic reprints) as part of his record. Byron's nine letters referring to the *Hebrew Melodies*, from which we cite where appropriate, may provide little to augment the details of Nathan's account, but at least they furnish confirming testimony.

What, then, would raise doubt about Nathan's story? In part, it was the vexation of Hobhouse and Moore at Byron's accepting the collaboration; but in their attempts to discredit Nathan as a composer, they substantiate rather than detract from Nathan's credibility.[28] More significant, perhaps, was the spat over publications rights; but whatever else may have resulted from the counterclaims of Murray and Nathan, it did nothing to disrupt the working relationship between the poet and composer, who continued to work on the arrangements for the second volume during the year following. Finally, there is nothing left to counter the reliability of Nathan's report but his own overeagerness to describe himself as a companion of the famous poet and his exaggerated claims about the antiquity of his music. The former requires no more of a corrective than a judicious tempering of Nathan's account. The latter problem, his claims about his musical sources, is complex and requires full attention.

Nathan owed Byron a great deal, and his debt grew. During that year separating the first and second volumes of *Hebrew Melodies*, he sold as sheet music his settings to twelve additional poems by Byron; in the years following the number increased to twenty.[29] As we have seen, the collaboration was by no means one-sided; Byron too owed a debt to Nathan, whose music, verve at the keyboard, and sensitivity to lyric made Byron's texts sound better than the poet could have hoped, given his lack of experience as a songwriter. What was it in Nathan's music that excited Byron? What made them think that their melodies would achieve a semblance of "Hebrewness"? Partly an imaginative adventure, this collaboration was still founded on musicological grounds far more extensive than has been recognized.

THE SOURCES OF
NATHAN'S MUSIC

To a great extent, the *Hebrew Melodies* mirror the conflicting claims of Nathan's several constituencies:

John Braham, whose name was signed to all the songs, though he wrote none.
Douglas Kinnaird, who assumed the role of promoter and sought to control publication.
Lord Byron, whom Nathan was obviously anxious to please.
Theater Critics, looking for thrills or neo-Purcell.
A Curious Public, accustomed to limited popular music.
The Jewish Community, sympathetic, but well aware of barriers to selling anything "Hebrew."

Despite these competing claims on Nathan's attention, he appears to have stuck to one main objective: His settings must achieve scholarly as well as financial success. To that end, Nathan got his friend, Robert Harding Evans of the *Times*, to write a preface for the first number of *Hebrew Melodies* titled "An Essay on the Music of the Hebrews," which reviewed biblical references to music, and made the modest claim that the Jewish music of 1815 preserved the "spirit" of the race's impassioned history. The essay was vetoed by Kinnaird.

Annoyed, apparently, by Nathan's intimacy with Byron, Kinnaird seems to have had time to realize how unprovable were Nathan's claims for his music's antiquity. He replaced Evans' essay with a terse introductory message, "signed" by Braham and Nathan, admitting that the "age and originality" of the tunes "must be left to conjecture." Evans' essay was printed by John Booth in 1816, but by then the damage had been done. The absence of even a gesture toward asserting the music's authenticity undermined Nathan's aims, and it has left a lasting impression that the *Hebrew Melodies* were never based on genuine motifs of synagogue practice, a charge which can now be refuted only in part. As an artist, he is an English composer working mostly in familiar popular modes. But as a researcher, he appears to have sought genuinely Hebrew source materials, although it is extremely difficult at this date to rediscover those sources, themselves already affected by the westernization of synagogue music.

Nathan's contemporaries held contradictory opinions on the music when it first appeared in 1815. Some charged inauthenticity:

The music now used in synagogues is of vague and arbitrary character, without a trace of the primitive melodies. In the present day, therefore, to set up pretensions to the restoration or imitation of genuine Hebrew music is trifling and irreverent. (William Roberts, *British Review,* August 1815)[30]

Nathan's efforts were appreciated by some of his contemporaries, however:

The harmonised airs . . . deserve particular notice from the delicacy of the melody and the science of the location of the notes. (*Critical Review,* April 1816)

In selecting melodies to suit the sentiment of the Poet, they [Braham and Nathan] have been extremely happy. The expression of some parts we feel to be so true and so powerful as strongly to remind us of our old favorite Purcell. (*Gentleman's Magazine,* June 1815)

Later nineteenth-century musicologists identified six of the tunes, a modest number among the twenty-nine songs. Unenchanted by Nathan, they appear to have worked halfway into volume one, then left off examining sources. One proof of this is that, after identifying the first six songs, Francis Cohen does not even bother to remark that "My Soul is Dark," the ninth song of the first volume, is obviously another adaptation of a Passover tune used in "Oh! Weep for Those" (the fourth song). The cursory result of these researches has gone unrevised for almost a century:

Though lacking in Hebraic character, six of the "Melodies" were used in the synagogue; probably four of these were derived from non-Jewish sources. The remainder of the music is very poor; and it has deservedly sunk into oblivion. (Francis Cohen)

The tunes, with the exception of those for *Chanukah* and *Pesach,* were not traditional at all. They are melodies created or adopted by various *chazzanim.* (Abraham Z. Idelsohn)

The tunes, partly derived from the Synagogue, were not well chosen; hence, though the poems have survived, the settings are forgotten . . . and my verdict is the same as Mr. Cohen's. (Israel Abrahams)[31]

Recent evaluations of the music, however, such as that by musicologist Eric Werner, have been much more positive:

The music does not presume to be written for the synagogue, but it was clearly art music based on *minhag ashkenaz* [Ashkenazic Tradition]. . . . It is true that the arrangement of the traditional tunes in the Byron songs leaves a good deal to be desired in craftsmanship, especially in the rather childishly set basses. But the style of English "domestic chamber music" was exactly of the same caliber and compositorial skill.[32]

To clarify: There are two issues here. One has to do with Nathan's skill as a composer, the other with the authenticity of his Jewish sources. Werner's judgment on both questions reflects a riper wisdom than that of Cohen, Idelsohn, or Abrahams. In retrospect, Nathan's settings are clearly a cut higher than his competition's in ambition, quality, and difficulty, even in the settings of the basses (one reviewer wished that the composer had created "more simplicity of accompaniment": *Critical Review,* April 1816). Joseph Slater puts this matter in a just light when he remarks that the music looks at least as workmanlike as Byron's lyrics.[33]

Nathan's settings also retain a significant trace of the synagogue tunes and practices of his time, as Werner points out. Whether it still be possible—or worthwhile—to seek and find sources for all the melodies he transcribed remains to be seen, but we have enough evidence to be sure that he did seriously intend to preserve what he was hearing in London and Canterbury synagogues. What he was likely to hear needs some explaining, however.

To understand the sources available to Nathan, one must first distinguish between two rich and complicated heritages. First, there were the traditional chants sung to melodies prescribed by the annotations to the biblical text, the Masora. Then there were also melodies sung to the non-biblical texts—a much freer mode. Nathan adapted from both, though chiefly from the latter.

The singing or chanting of the Masoretic text is prescribed by notations above and below the textual lines. Different regions of the Judaic world assign differing values to the signs, and the exact modulations of the voice can vary, not only from region to region, but also depending on the occasion and the context in which particular signs are found—that is, their relation to other notations to the same text. Nevertheless, the notations to the Masora stem from a recognized set of relationships between sign and sound, a sort of solfeggio (do-re-mi), complicated, but suitable for transcription and memorization. One cannot, of course, transcribe into Western musical notations the quarter-tone steps so characteristic of cantillation, but the general shape of the melody can be recorded thus. Let us look at the one known example of Nathan's having used the notations of the Masora as a source for the *Hebrew Melodies*.

Previously unidentified by musicologists, the source for "Jephtha's Daughter" can be recognized as a version of the melody belonging to the Song of Songs, or *Shir Hashirim*. By comparing the title (in Hebrew) with the first line of the text, you will be able to discriminate the added signs, which appear sometimes above, sometimes below the text, as a guide to chanting. These signs form a sort of language themselves. They come in certain patterns and with certain options of variability in those patterns, but not with others. For example, the commalike sign under the first character (reading, of course, from right to left) is followed by a sign (again, below the line) looking like a reverse comma. The first sign is called *mercha* and the second *tipcha*. The two signs form a sort of partnership, and though one may find

THE SONG OF SOLOMON, CHAP. I.

THE song of songs, which *is* Solomon's. 2 Let him kiss me with the kisses of his mouth · for thy love *is* better than wine.

שִׁיר וּ,שִׁירִים א
שִׁיר הַשִּׁירִים אֲשֶׁר לִשְׁלֹמֹה ׃ ² יִשָּׁקֵנִי
מִנְּשִׁיקוֹת פִּיהוּ כִּי־טוֹבִים דֹּדֶיךָ
מִיָּיִן ׃

tipcha in other contexts, *mercha* will always be followed by it.

The actual pattern of the chanting may be practiced by the student for the rabbinate, such as Nathan himself was at one time. Thus, the following "scale" might be used by one rehearsing the *Shir Hashirim:*

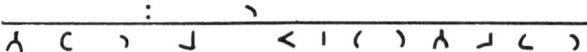

Here is a transcription of the beginning of this cantillation, based upon the melodic figures still being chanted in some Middle Eastern communities:[34]

Mer - cha   tip-cha   mu-nach et-nach-ta

Note that the words under the melody are *not* the text of the Song of Songs, but a transliteration of the names of the signs (*mercha, tipcha,* etc).

This particular melody[35] seems to have provided the formula Nathan used to write "Jephtha's Daughter":

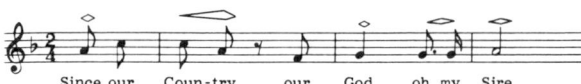

Since our Coun-try, our God, oh my Sire

In addition to taking the melody from the cantillation of the Masora, Nathan appears, in this song and in many others, to have come as close as he possibly could to creating the quarter-tone steps and cadenzas characteristic of solo cantillation. Sometimes he invites such interpretations by providing "ad lib" notes, as he does in "We sate down and wept," where the harmonic context is expressly modal, and seems more related to the motets of Lassus than the major/minor scales of Beethoven. At other times, he simply writes in cadenzes or elaborations, as in the 1815–1816 version of "Sun of the Sleepless!" In "Oh Snatch'd Away in Beauty's Bloom" one hears the conflict between the harmonic minor and melodic minor generating some effects (as in the repetition of "the wild cypress wave," p. 41) that could be interpreted by the individual artist in a cantorial manner. Indeed, such was most probably the rendition of John Braham in the first public performance of *Hebrew Melodies,* for Braham, renowned for his improvisations, was himself a cantor. In "The Wild Gazelle," to add one more example, the repetition of "on Salem's Throne" (p. 23) seems to set up one of those contexts in which a Braham might easily introduce, perhaps not a quarter-tone step, but a slide or slur which would satisfy the anticipation of his audience for the piquancy of "Hebrew melody."

In addition to melodies and techniques of cantillation for biblical texts, Nathan used melodies written for non-biblical texts: *Kaddish, Lekha dodi, Eli tzayan,* etc. These melodies could be and were composed by anyone wishing to contribute to, amplify, or change the flavor of the service. Naturally, some tried to establish traditional melodies, like the *Ma'oz tzur,* a Chanukah tune Nathan adapted for "On Jordan's Banks." But every community of Jews developed some of its own distinctive melodies, and new contributions had found their way into synagogues throughout the Continent and Great Britain in the eighteenth century. Western major and minor modes, which had invaded synagogue practice already in the fourteenth and fifteenth centuries, had stabilized by this time. So the music Nathan would have heard in the synagogues in London and Canterbury was without doubt not just of "vague and arbitrary" origin (to use Roberts' phrase) but thoroughly corrupt, from a musicological standpoint.[36] In a London synagogue in 1814, he would have been more likely to hear a tune that had come from the English countryside than one the Jews had sung "before the destruction of the temple." Here, for example, is a passage from a melody sung in the Sephardic congregation in London at the time Nathan was conducting his research:

(Aguilar, I, 5)

Le chah do di   Il krat   ha lah

Had Nathan been searching for sounds of ethnic flavor, such a melody would not have come into his collection. Though he concentrated on the songs of the Ashkenazic Jews, Nathan collected only a few with distinctive ethnicity. We know, too, that he complained that it took him much longer than anticipated to "adapt" the music, which suggests that he did not understand precisely the limits of his "raw material," and that he struggled much harder than Cohen or Idelsohn acknowledge to preserve the tunes he had transcribed.

Here is a list of the contents of the first number of *Hebrew*

Melodies, together with identifying remarks about the sources:

She Walks in Beauty	—A "former *Lakha dodi* of London Synagogues" (Cohen).
The Harp the Monarch Minstrel Swept	—Tune (*Ya'aleh tahunen*) from the eve of Yom Kippur (Werner).
If that High World	—Tune sung to *Kaddish* after reading of the Law (Cohen).
The Wild Gazelle	—English folk song adapted to *Yig dal* (Cohen).
Oh! Weep for Those	—Northern folk song adapted into Passover service (Cohen).
On Jordan's Banks	—13th c. German hymn; *Ma'oz tzur,* Chanukah tune (Werner).
Jephtha's Daughter	—Unidentified by Cohen or others, but clearly a melody *given* before the text; it may be *Shir Hashirim,* sung to Song of Songs. Related versions in some dozen Middle Eastern communities (Douglass).
Oh Snatch'd Away in Beauty's Bloom	—Unidentified by Cohen or others, but bearing striking resemblance to an *Eli tziyan* recorded by Werner; see note to song (Douglass).
My Soul is Dark	—Unidentified by Cohen or others, but clearly another adaptation of the Passover tune of "Oh! Weep for Those" (Douglass).
I saw thee Weep	—Unidentified.
Thy Days are done	—Unidentified by Cohen or others, but bearing striking resemblance to an older *Missinai* tune of the High Holidays recorded by Werner; see note to song (Douglass).
It is the Hour	—Unidentified.

The omission of Evans' essay and the subsequent skepticism of scholars like Cohen and Idelsohn changed the expectations of critics. Nathan lost his point, or loses it now, anyway, if genuine antiquity is the criterion. But he clearly did record tunes he had heard and arrange them in his songs. Even the second volume (1816), which does not contain a single *identified* tune, almost certainly makes continued use of that research—more extensively than we can yet document.

The length to which Nathan was willing to go in order to preserve the music becomes clear when one opens the first volume to the first song, "She Walks in Beauty." This song remained one of Nathan's and Byron's favorites, and it was kept in the lead position when Nathan issued the second edition beginning in 1824. He claims here (emphasizing the scholarly pretensions of the project) that he could not choose between two very similar versions of a tune (identified as *Lekha dodi* by Cohen) heard in different synagogues. The antiquity of the tune is extremely doubtful, for the text of *Lekha dodi,* sung at every regular Friday night service, has produced as many melodies as any, and this particular version has no recorded history prior to Nathan's era. But Nathan treated this tune with a reverence that even led him into mild trouble.

The trouble is the usual one faced by arrangers trying to reconcile a given text with a given melody. Notice what happens when you sing the opening phrase:

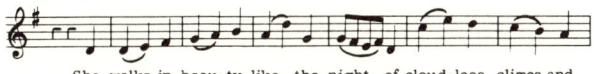
She walks in beau-ty like the night_of cloud-less climes and

The turn in bar 6 interferes with the natural resting point of "night" (with its long vowel), forcing the sense slightly. This turn, which occurs in both versions of the tune, is one of its significant features. Nathan could not begin the next line ("Of cloudless . . .") on the downbeat, for that would have skewed the accented syllable off from the accented part of the bar. So he was stuck in a mildly awkward moment in the song. Notice that he gets out of the trouble when he sets the next two lines to the same melody:

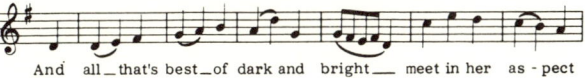
And all_that's best_of dark and bright_ meet in her as-pect

Because "Meet" is stressed, he can let "bright" finish the phrase. There can be no doubt that this was a compromise for Nathan—in *Musurgia Vocalis* he made clear that all good composers let stressed words fall on the accented part of the bar.[37]

Another such compromise may be found in "On Jordan's Banks." Again, try to sing the first few bars:

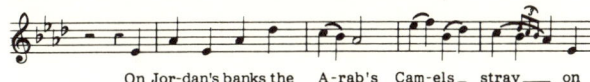
On Jor-dan's banks the A-rab's Cam-els_ stray__ on

The musical phrasing divides possessor ("Arab's") from possessed ("camels"). This particular tune, the *Ma'oz tzur,* a thirteenth-century hymn of German origin, is most familiar as a Chanukah melody, but it also provided the setting for a chorale by Martin Luther: "So weiß ich eins was mich erfreut." Sure to be recognized, it could not be altered to fit the lyric. A good singer can smooth over this bar—but only a *good* singer. Throughout the volume, Nathan, seeking to preserve the original music, encounters occasional awkwardness.

We have no reason to suppose Nathan wrote other "Hebrew" melodies out of his head without relying on research; indeed, we have good reason to suppose the opposite. The fact that the tunes were sung in the synagogue does not, of course, necessarily give the songs a genuinely "Hebrew" character. Clearly, Nathan responded to currently fashionable Italian and German motifs. But there is also evidence that he adapted cantillatory ornaments and the harmony of chants for his settings, as in the "Vision of Belshazzar" and "Thy Days Are Done." A comparison of his practice here with his later compositions also shows that he employed such ornaments and harmonic devices almost exclusively for the *Hebrew Melodies*. One finds cadenzas and harmonic shifts of a different type in Nathan's "Why are you wandering here, I pray?" and other songs for Kenney's libretti. The matter of Nathan's appropriating a Jewish "style," we shall address in the concluding section of this introduction.

Finally, the musicological purity of the project, though not an insignificant matter, is less important than the impression of ethnic authenticity that was conjured in Byron's mind and in the minds of that audience who heard John Braham's concert performance at Drury Lane. In the competitive field of "national airs," Byron and Nathan's *Hebrew Melodies* would have the distinction of having been accomplished in true collaboration, and the composer's use of Jewish themes did not need be limited to inherited tunes, any more than the poet's use of the Bible needed to be limited to paraphrase.

Identity and Tradition in Byron's Lyrics

We know that Nathan made an impression on Byron with his expertise at the keyboard and his accomplishments as a vocalist and composer. Byron heard Nathan's music first in his rooms at the Albany, and he was soon engaged in working out an array of Jewish themes. In the early cantos of *Childe Harold*, in *Lara* and *The Corsair*, Byron had already developed the role of the outcast, the exile, a persona that would fit well into the historical Jewish context. Byron's assumption of Jewish identity was immediately noted in contemporary reviews: "The present state of the Jewish people—expatriated—dispersed—trodden down—contemned —afforded the noble poet a very fine subject; and . . . he has not neglected to avail himself of it." (*Christian Observer*, August 1815). Indeed, so fully did the Byronic persona represent the agonizing dilemma of Jewish identity that Heinrich Heine proclaimed Byron his true cousin and kindred spirit: "He was the only person with whom I felt myself related, and we may well have had many things in common. . . . I always consorted comfortably with Byron as with a best friend, my full equal" (To Moses Moser, 25 June 1824).[38]

Heine was in the midst of his *Harzreise* when he learned of Byron's death at Missolonghi (April 1824). He had already translated passages from *Childe Harold* and *Manfred* and some of Byron's lyrics, including "Fare Thee Well." Byron's *Hebrew Melodies* inspired Heine to write his *Hebräische Melodien* (1851), which are narrative rather than lyric but not without echoes of Byron's themes. From his sickbed in Paris, Heine recollected the sway of Byron's influence: "I was young, my friend, twenty-five years, when my breast echoed with the wild melancholy of Byron."[39] Although Heine complained that Byron's spirit was too splenetic, still he recognized in the *Hebrew Melodies* the voice of an intimate friend and relative, "Vetter Byron."

Heinrich Heine's sense of kinship with the Byronic persona may provide useful testimony of Byron's Jewish affinity, but it does not explain how the poet accomplished that emphatic voice. Byron, even after he yielded to the persuasion of Kinnaird and Braham, did not immediately welcome the task. As a favor to Kinnaird, he forwarded those five or six poems. Most he had written during the past five or six months. Only one, "Oh! weep for those that wept by Babel's stream," was actually composed, as Kinnaird recognized, in response to Nathan's plan. "Sun of the Sleepless" Kinnaird also thought beautiful, and he promised that "the verses not to be set to music . . . shall be return'd uncopied to you." The other poems from this first offering must have seemed to Kinnaird ill-suited to the *Hebrew Melodies:* "It is the hour" and "Francisca" were verses Byron later used to introduce *Parisina* (22 January 1816), his notorious narrative of incest and revenge; "I speak not—I trace not—I breathe not thy name" was addressed to his half sister Augusta Leigh (4 May 1814); "She Walks in Beauty" described Anne Wilmot's appearance in a spangled mourning gown (12 June 1814).[40]

In less than four days Nathan brought his settings to Byron. Even these first poems, seemingly miscast in the context of the *Hebrew Melodies,* took on a significant Jewish modality when adapted by Nathan, and Byron was impressed, though also amused by Nathan's simplistic inquiries on the meaning of a poetic image. Nathan's own account of these conversations during their collaboration reveal that he was not as naive as he pretended. Indeed, he repeatedly used his simple queries about interpreting Byron's poem as a disguised occasion to explain something of Jewish customs and lore. His role in acquainting Byron with the Jewish tradition is crucial to the understanding of the *Hebrew Melodies*. Although his poetic insight was limited, Nathan gave the poems a musical interpretation that impressed Byron for literal fidelity to the language and insistent Jewish ethnicity. Intrigued by the rhythms, the poet began to search for themes to follow Nathan's musical suggestions. At the end of their first month of collaboration, Byron wrote to Annabella Milbanke: "Kinnaird . . . applied to me to write words for a musical composer who is going to publish the *real old undisputed Hebrew melodies,* which are beautiful & to which David & the prophets actually sang the 'songs of Zion'—& I have done nine or ten on the sacred model—partly from Job &c. & partly from my own imagination; but I hope a little better than Sternhold & Hopkins." (20 October 1814)

Byron sought to overcome the cultural disparity, as well as the personal pretension of a goy assuming a "Hebrew" voice, to achieve a semblance of Jewishness in his lyrics. He objected to the metrical *Psalms* (1547) of Thomas Sternhold and John Hopkins, not because they were too English or too Christian, but simply because they were the work of clumsy versifiers. Once Nathan had acquainted him with the music and his plan to introduce the *Hebrew Melodies* into the popular vogue for "national airs," Byron tried to shape his Hebrew matter in a way that would suit Nathan's notions of the historical color and ritual fervor of ancient Temple liturgies.

To be sure, the "national airs" succeeded more in nourishing sentiment and evoking stereotypes, less in adhering faithfully to ethnic and folk traditions. Byron, as we have seen, was a sincere admirer of Thomas Moore's poignant lyrics, for Moore's melancholy and nostalgia were informed by strength and integrity protesting against a history of Irish oppression and subjugation. Byron had mocked Sidney Smythe, Viscount Strangford, for the "harmonious fustian" of his *Poems, from the Portuguese* (1803), accusing him of "false pretence" in "dressing Camoëns in a suit of lace" and teaching "the Lusian bard to copy Moore" (*English Bards and Scotch Reviewers*, 11. 295–308, 921–922). Among those who had endeavored to appropriate biblical motifs, "Sepulchral Grahame" is chastised for his "dull devotions" and "mangled prose." In *Sabbath Walks* and *Biblical Pictures,* Grahame "boldly pilfers from the Pentateuch; / And, undisturb'd by conscientious qualms, / Perverts the prophets, and purloins the Psalms" (11. 318–326). With gradations from praise to scorn, Byron evaluated several other translations and adaptations of national songs. William Herbert, he conceded, managed to "wield Thor's hammer" (11. 511–512) in *Select Icelandic Poetry* (1804, 1806). Clearly, Byron distinguished a right and wrong way for engaging the "national air."

His conviction that Moore's way was the right way, Byron reveals again and again in his collaboration with Nathan, and his contemporaries immediately recognized the similarity between "The Harp the Monarch Minstrel Swept" and Moore's "The Harp that once, thro' Tara's halls." But Byron was not content to follow Moore's example, no matter how moving and emotive his lyric evocation of Irish themes. Byron sought text and context for his persona, his virtuoso act of literary self-projection. Saul and David, joined by all persecuted Jewish people, become "Byronic heroes." His success in providing a powerful lyric evocation of the Jewish spirit may well be measured by the vehement anti-Semitism raised by critics who saw the *Hebrew Melodies* as an assault on Christianity. In the reviews, the name of George Gordon, Lord Byron, as "poet laureate to the synagogue," was linked to Lord George Gordon, the "traitor Jew." Augusta Leigh had rightly predicted that Byron would be called "a Jew," but she could not have anticipated that critics would charge the "Jew" with even more malicious opprobrium than Alexander Pope leveled against Edmund Curll in the *Dunciad.*

The reviewer for the *British Critic* (June 1815) begins his account of the *Hebrew Melodies* by recalling from the *Miscellanies* of Swift and Pope "A strange but true Relation how Mr. E. Curll out of an extraordinary desire was converted by certain eminent Jews."

We had just laid down the humorous account of the apostacy of Edmund Curll, and of his subsequent circumcision, when Lord Byron's Hebrew Melodies presented themselves to our view. That worthy bookseller, after having libelled all mankind, is represented by his biographer, no less a man than Swift himself, to have first fallen a victim to the malice of Mr. Pope, and afterwards to have turned Jew, having undergone all the ceremonies of a regular initiation. Having given the name of the historian, our readers will probably see sufficient reason why we should rather recommend the perusal than transcribe the detail of the various transactions which attended the sickness and apostacy of this celebrated literary character.

After suggesting an economic coercion of proselytizing Jews, rendering "the Society for the Propagation of Judaism among Christians . . . rather more successful in its endeavors, though not so loud in its pretensions, as the society for the Propagation of Christianity among the Jews," the reviewer goes on to cite the case of Lord George Gordon:

The last noble Lord who became an open and a professed convert to the Jewish faith was Lord George Gordon of turbulent memory, and as he was probably as admirable a divine as he was a politician, we cannot doubt the excellence of his motives or the strength of his example.

As political divine, Lord George Gordon first presented himself as Protestant hero, opposing the Catholic relief act and arousing the mob that pillaged Catholic homes and chapels and set fire to Newgate prison (Gordon Riots, June 1780); supporting the Dutch against Emperor Joseph (November 1782); celebrating his excommunication from the Church of England for refusing to bear witness in an ecclesiastical suit (1786); then defending Cagliostro against the persecutions of Marie Antoinette in the Diamond Necklace affair (1787); finally, as champion of the peace, converting to Judaism and calling upon all Jewish moneylenders not to lend money for warfare (1788). He also attempted to arouse Newgate prisoners to protest criminal laws, capital punishment, and prison conditions. Charged with slander and sedition, he was imprisoned in Newgate, where he continued his Judaic devotions until he died, singing "Ça ira" (1 November 1793). Lord George Gordon's schemes have been maligned as mad but also defended as truly dedicated to freedom. While the reviewer snidely implies the former, Byron might well have found reason enough in the latter to accept the comparison as an unintended compliment.

When John Cam Hobhouse was imprisoned in Newgate (14 December 1819) for his political pamphleteering, Byron defends the call for "Constitutional amelioration of long abuses" and lists his friend among the genteel reformers: "Lord George Gordon—and Wilkes—and Burdett—and Horne Tooke—were all men of education—and courteous deportment—so is Hobhouse" (to John Murray, 21 February 1820).

The reviewer, after introducing the precedent of Edmund Curll and Lord George Gordon, ridicules *Hebrew Melodies* as the declaration of Byron's Jewish initiation rites upon accepting "the proffered chaplet of his Jewish brethren." Ignorant of "the secrets of Duke's Place," he pretends not to judge the motives of Nathan and Braham, whether prompted by piety or profit "to assist the devotion of the synagogue, or to increase the trade of the shop"; the motives of Byron he condemns as either ridiculous (if sincere) or hypocritical. The reviewer tolerantly sanctions the right of London Jews to keep their devotions in the Jewry (which crosses at Aldgate to the Jewish shops in Duke's Place, whence the euphemism for Jewry), but he denounces Jewish partisanship by "a peer of the realm":

We . . . confess our surprise that a peer of the realm should so far identify himself with the worthy inhabitants of Duke's Place, as to be hawked about in a species of co-partnership with the *ci-de-vant* Mr. Abraham, (*per aphaeresis* Mr. Braham) and Mr. Nathan. If these latter gentlemen, in the fervour of devotional attachment to the memory of their forefathers, and the glories of their ancient days, are desirous of proclaiming the beauties of the songs of Sion in a strange land, they are at full liberty to indulge the warmth of their affections, we respect their motives, we honour even their prejudices; if, on the other hand, profit be their object, let them reap the harvest of their industry, and enjoy the fruits of a monopoly, to which, as Jews, they are so fully entitled. But let not a peer of the realm, who is *ex professo,* at least, a Christian, enter into so close a literary union with these worthy gentlemen as to expose himself to the unpleasant dilemma of being supposed either to entertain an attachment to the Jewish cause, which in him would at best be ridiculous, or to feign that affection towards a sacred object, to which his heart is in reality a stranger.

Having given Jewish music and poetry back to the Jews for their own indulgence, the reviewer goes on to argue that in a Christian realm the reading of the Old Testament, and the poetry derived from it, should be informed by Christian piety. Because Byron had established himself in his earlier poetry as a "stranger" to religious devotion, the reviewer finds him guilty here of imposture and impropriety. He won the amused approval of his critic only when he broke from "his Hebrew fetters" and "abandoned the Judaism of his task" in such poems as "I saw thee Weep" and "It is the Hour." Byron modestly claimed his lyrics "a little better than Sternhold & Hopkins"; he was charged with offering something vilely worse. Not surprisingly, the more ardent of the proto-Zionist poems, "Oh! Weep for Those" and "On Jordan's Banks," are the ones this reviewer cites as especially offensive. He then proceeds to set forth, in contrast to Byron's "uncouth" and "wretched" poems, the finer accomplishments of Thomas Morell, Reginald Heber, Brady and Tate; even Sternhold and Hopkins, "these twin votaries of pious doggrel are actually beyond the noble Lord."

In a similar attack, William Roberts, in the *British Review* (August 1815), begins by scorning the conventionality of "national airs"—"minstrels, and languishing maidens, the big bright tear, the dark blue eye, lover's vows, and tender glances." In charging Byron with "mental prostitution" in service to Nathan and Braham, Roberts does not withhold snide reference to the moneylenders: "A young Lord is seldom the better for meddling with the Jews." These Jews, however, have gained from an "uninspired" poet only his "perfect vacuity of poetical thought and feeling." Roberts also raises the example of Lord George Gordon: "We do not think that Lord Byron makes a better figure with his Jewish minstrelsy, than Lord George Gordon with his rabbinical beard; and if he persists in this perversion of his genius, we shall really be tempted to think him as little right in his senses." Byron should learn from the Holy Scriptures "not how to write on Jewish topics, but how 'To shame the doctrine of the Sadducees'." The main fault of his biblical poetry is that he fails "to become a humble believer" and he writes without "the true scriptural elevation of mind." The Muse of the "sacred song" must not be allowed to mix in "bad company": "He must have nothing to do with those Moabitish melodies, fitted only for the high places and groves of Baal, and which the virgin daughter of Zion cannot hear without pollution." Byron profanes the holy ground with fatuous love lyrics and ignores that divine love song, the Song of Songs, the "sublime and mystic allegory" of the bridal union of Jehovah and the true Church.

The reviewer of the *Christian Observer* (August 1815), already quoted, expressed the propriety of Byron's taking the part of the downtrodden Jew, but he found the proto-Zionist polemics too aggressive and censured "Oh! Weep for Those" because the lines "ungracefully confound the present state of the Jews with the Babylonian captivity." Josiah Condor, in the *Eclectic Review* (July 1815), writes with some outrage that "in one respect alone they are Jewish poems." They are anti-Christian. He points particularly to the accusations raised in "On the Day of the Destruction of Jerusalem by Titus": "They are as *Jewish,* in opposition to every thing *Christian,* as Messrs. Nathan and Braham could have desired." Condor doesn't sense the absurdity of his claim that "in order to sweep the harp of David, a man needs be not only pre-eminently a poet, but emphatically a Christian." He judges Byron by the Anglican tradition of "sacred poetry" and finds him wanting. The critical reception of the *Hebrew Melodies* was divided on the question of the Hebrew identity of the poems, but the conclusion was largely the same. Whether the critic recognized that the poet had taken the part of the oppressed Jew and championed the Zionist cause, or merely saw that he had not followed the accepted norms for adapting biblical texts, Byron was criticized for abandoning the proper Christian model for the "sacred song."

Although his critics thus measured the *Hebrew Melodies* in terms of the generic expectations provided by the tradition of "sacred songs," Byron himself created his "Hebrew" melodies more from his own perception of Old Testament history and drama. His idea of "sacred song" had no debt to pay to Anglican models. Models he had, but these were the "national airs" of Moore, which Byron chose to inform with his own proto-Zionist fervor and his own speculations on God and immortality. It was unfortunate that Moore responded in ill-tempered rivalry, denouncing Nathan for "puffing off his Jewish wares in all sorts of quackish ways."⁴¹ Byron began his collaboration with Nathan not knowing that Moore had previously proposed to James Power a volume of *Sacred Songs*. He candidly acknowledged Moore's superiority in song. Byron learned to imitate that verve of proud nationalism which resounds in the *Irish Melodies,* but Moore himself was not able to match such a feeling in his *Sacred Songs*. For one thing, Moore did not take up the Zionist cause. Nor did he hold to his role as "sweet singer of Israel." His themes include St. Jerome's reply, "Who is the Maid," to the imputations of his love affair with Paula. A similar piece of piety triumphant over sins of the flesh is Moore's air on "Sinful Mary's Tears." The most jubilant in the series of sixteen poems is Miriam's Song." Moore takes the scene from the song of Moses following the escape across the Red Sea, when Miriam, like Jephtha's daughter, "took a timbrel in her hand; and all the women went out after her, with timbrels and dances" (Exodus 15:20). Three times Moore repeats the lines "Sound loud the Timbrel o'er Egypt's dark sea! / Jehovah has triumph'd,—his people are free." Moore's elegiac lament "Weep not for those" scarcely competes with its parallel in *Hebrew Melodies*. Moore's songs were set—no, were spliced—to strains borrowed from Mozart, Beethoven, and Haydn, as well as to airs of Avison and Stevenson. The resulting mélange, however, managed to please those critics looking for traditional "sacred songs."

The music of Moore's *Sacred Songs* was typical of the makeshift arrangements for "national melodies," unlike Byron's collaboration with Nathan in which a set of tunes had been gathered for the project, and poet and composer listened to each other and traded on each other's rhythms and motifs. By the time Byron bade his farewell to Nathan, and to England, he had given him ten poems based on the "sacred model"; twelve on historical, speculative, and proto-Zionist themes; and a miscellany of seven love songs and elegiac laments. In searching through the Old Testament and Josephus's *Antiquities of the Jews,* Byron had little difficulty identifying "the wandering outlaw of his own dark mind," or the "heart . . . form'd for softness—warp'd to wrong," such types as he could absorb into his poetic persona of brooding melancholy. He had already created Harold, Lara, and Conrad, and his exposition in *Hebrew Melodies* of Saul, Herod, and Belshazzar prepared the way for the creation of a Byronic hero caught up in dark spiritual conflict. The success of *Manfred* and the more explicitly biblical works, *Cain* and *Heaven and Earth,* prompted Goethe's regret that Byron had not lived "to secure his vocation *(seine Bestimmung)*." Goethe emphasized the Hebraic affinity in praising Byron's *Bestimmung:* "To dramatise the *Old* Testament. What a subject, under his hands, would the Tower of Babel have been!"⁴²

THE "SACRED MODEL"

Touched with mad spells of gloomy torment, trespassing mortal laws to delve in necromancy, yet rising defiant and unawed to confront death: such a description would suit Byron's Manfred but it fits as well his appropriation of Saul for three of the *Hebrew Melodies:* "My Soul is Dark," Thou whose Spell can raise the Dead," and "Warriors and Chiefs!" In "Thy Days are done," Byron praises the fallen warrior, borrowing from David's tribute to the heroism of Saul and Jonathan. Suffering and the looming threat of divine vengeance inform his adaptation from the Psalms and his account of the destruction of the Sennacherib. Byron did not adulate, rather he drew from his "sacred model" sketches of a troubled theodicy and of individuals caught in tribulation. He gives a proud voice to Jephtha's Daughter confronting the conditions of her father's vow. In putting on "Jewishness," he also puts on the spiritual agony of the soul whose vision is trapped in selfishness or whose worldly pleasures rankle. Not only Saul, but also Eliphaz and Belshazzar appear in such lyric portraits.

After Saul had been set up as king over Israel, he defeated the Amalekites yet disobeyed the divine command to kill King Agag and destroy his property. David was then anointed by the king-maker Samuel. When the Spirit of the Lord thus passed from Saul to David, "an evil spirit" came to possess Saul. Only David's music had the power to soothe the tormented king: "And it came to pass, when the evil spirit from God was upon Saul, that David took an harp, and played with his hand: so Saul was refreshed, and was well, and the evil spirit departed from him" (I Samuel 16:23). In the first stanza of Byron's poem, Saul not only confesses his sickness, "My soul is dark," he also explains how music may effect its cure by bleeding the pent-up emotions: the hope, buried within, may be released; the unshed tear, scalding the brain, may be allowed to flow. In the second stanza, Saul explains that the art itself must penetrate the emotional depths to work as catharsis. When he tells David to "bid the strain be wild and deep," Nathan repeats a bit of stereotypical "wildness" from his setting of "The Wild Gazelle." In the agony of his disease, Saul calls desperately for the purgation: "I must weep, / Or else this heavy heart will burst" it must "break at once—or yield to song." Byron leaves Saul in the very dilemma of his urgent appeal to David. Nathan, however, allows for the musical efficacy of David's song when he repeats the final phrase, "or yield to song," first rising and then descending to the harmonic close.

"Thou whose Spell can raise the Dead" follows Saul through the trial created when the army of the Philistines marched against Israel. Saul was afraid, and he longed for Samuel's wise counsel. But Samuel was dead. Saul therefore turned to the Witch of Endor who could communicate with the dead through her familiar. At Samuel's behest, Saul had outlawed necromancy. Now, in disguise, he secretly violates his own law and visits the witch by night (I Samuel 28:7–19). For the voices of Saul, the Witch, and the Ghost of Samuel, Byron uses a four-beat line with rhythmic shifts of amphimacer and iambs, or trochees and amphimacer. Following Saul's request and the Witch's conjuration in four terse lines, Byron then turns to iambic pentameter for his Gothic description of the reanimated corpse: "Earth yawned; he stood the centre of a cloud." The six lines of morbid detail close with two dactyls and two iambs, "Shrunken and sinewless, and ghastly bare." For the voice of the Ghost, he returns to the four-beat line. Here he holds closely to the biblical text, altering principally to heighten dramatic effect. Like the conjured Astarte who tells Manfred, "Tomorrow ends thine earthly ills. Farewell!" (II, iv, 151–52), the Ghost of Samuel pronounces Saul's doom, "Fare thee well, but for a day; / Then we mix our mouldering clay." The biblical Samuel had said, "Tomorrow shalt thou and thy sons be with me." That the curse also descends upon the sons of Saul, Byron emphasizes in the final lines: "Crownless, breathless, headless fall, / Son and sire, the House of Saul."

Just as this poem was metrically the most complex in the sequence, so too it was musically the most elaborate. It includes the only trio in the 1815–16 edition (the trio became a quintet in the later revised edition). Nathan adapted High Holyday styles and gave the music his most thorough Handelian treatment. "I felt a difficulty in the composition," Nathan admitted, "because I saw the height of beauty his lines had reached, and I trembled lest he had soared too high for my imagination's *accompaniment*." After Nathan rehearsed his composition, he was relieved to find that Byron was so pleased that he began repeating the ghostly *recitativo,* "Why is my sleep disquieted," claiming "the passage would haunt him." The next morning, Byron told Nathan he had indeed been visited and had "greeted some early intruder with what he could recollect of the passage." Byron explained that this was no "interview with Lady Endor, or with Samuel's vision:—the intruder that greeted me was no hobgoblin, I assure you, it was only Douglas Kinnaird" (*FP,* 54–55).

This song was soon to attain the added distinction of marking the break between Nathan and Kinnaird. As part of the drawing-room entertainment, Nathan recalls, Kinnaird and his "beautiful hostess" joined Nathan in singing "a trio of one of my Hebrew Melodies" ("Thou whose Spell can raise the Dead" and "In the Valley of Waters" were the only two melodies Nathan had harmonized for trio). Hinting at a situation perhaps similar to Rowe's *The Fair Penitent* (the participants are otherwise unnamed), Nathan tells us that he sang tenor, Calista sang soprano, "and her Lothario took the *bass* part." Nathan then concluded with the ghostly curse as solo aria. The wine, "the sweet singing of his fair companion," the presence of "the first poet of the day," conspired to make this Lothario "fancy himself *greater* than the *greatest* of the *great.*" Nathan's word for Kinnaird's behavior was "officious." On this occasion, chagrined that his kept mistress as well as Byron took such delight in Nathan's music, he became even more officious than usual:

forgetting all gentle manly feeling and propriety of hospitality, he turned towards me with an air of consequence peculiarly his own, and vociferated with all the stentorian power of his lungs, "Mr. Nathan, I expect a——a—— that——a—— you bring out these Melodies in good style ——a——a—— and bear in mind, that——a——a—— his Lordship's name does not suffer from scantiness——a——a——in their publication." (*FP,* 93)

Byron must have seen Nathan wince at Kinnaird's suggestion, almost an accusation, that he might be stingy and profit-mongering in his negotiations with C. Richards for the printing of *Hebrew Melodies.* In fact, Nathan spared no effort to make this a splendid folio: Edward Blore, an architect skilled in Gothic design (he sketched York and Peterborough for John Britton's *English Cathedrals* and planned the exterior for Sir Walter Scott's estate in Abbotsford), provided Nathan with a noble Gothic title page and a florid dedication page. As soon as Kinnaird left the room, "Lord Byron . . . seized the opportunity of shaking me most cordially by the hand . . . and in a low voice said. 'Do not mind him, he's a fool!'" The following morning, when Nathan called on Byron at Piccadilly Terrace, Byron repeated his trust in the planned edition: "'Nathan, do not suffer that capricious fool to lead you into more expence than is absolutely necessary; bring out the work to your own taste: I have no ambition to gratify, beyond that of proving useful to you'" (*FP,* 94). Granted, this is Nathan fondly recollecting what he no doubt wanted to hear from Byron. But his portrait of Kinnaird seems true-to-life. William Jerdan, editor of the *Sun,* describes a similarly "officious" Kinnaird, who interrupted Coleridge's reading from *Remorse* with the declaration that he had "'listened to enough of your nonsense.'"[43] Nathan had already experienced considerable rudeness at these dinners with Kinnaird. When he visited Kinnaird that previous November, John Cam Hobhouse sided with his host and would not conceal his anti-Semitic indignation that he must dine with "a Jew for whom Ld. Byron has written words to Jewish melodies": "we had a scene—which is a good lesson against keeping [Kinnaird's keeping a "hostess"]—poor B was taken to task for making Mr. N impudent by shaking hands with him" (26 November 1814).[44]

"Warriors and Chiefs!," the third song of Saul, takes the apostate king into his last battle. The Ghost of Samuel has foretold his death. Knowing that his defeat by the Philistines is inevitable, Saul bravely dons his armor and calls upon his soldiers and sons to make a bold stand. The biblical Saul speaks only to call upon his sword-bearer: "Draw thy sword, and thrust me through therewith; lest these uncircumcised come and thrust me through, and abuse me" (I Samuel 31:4). The biblical verse provides the second stanza:

Thou who art bearing my buckler and bow,
Should the soldiers of Saul look away from the foe,
Stretch me that moment in blood at thy feet!
Mine be the doom which they dared not to meet.

The first stanza is the call to battle; the last stanza is the farewell to those who will fall. Byron thus amplifies Saul's final speech into an heroic reaffirmation of honor and fortitude, as dramatic as the death of Conrad or Lara. In Nathan's account, Byron sought to redeem Saul from his degeneracy as "the coward whom supernatural evils have worn down" by reinstating the "originally brave and estimable man." A martial introduction and incremental march rhythms are developed by Nathan to provide the appropriate setting.

"Thy Days are done" echoes lines from David's tribute at the death of Saul. When Saul's sword-bearer feared to slay his chief, "Saul took a sword, and fell on it." Thus when the Philistines overwhelmed Saul's defense upon Mount Gilboa, they found only his corpse. After the slaughter of the Amalekites, David calls upon one of the soldiers who claims that he found Saul still alive and begging for an end to his agony: "He said unto me again, Stand I pray thee, upon me, and slay me: for anguish is come upon me, because my life is yet whole in me. So I stood upon him, and slew him, because I was sure that he could not live after that he was fallen: and I took the crown that was upon his head, and the bracelet that was on his arm, and have brought them hither unto my lord" (II Samuel 1:6–10). At odds with the account already told, the soldier debases Saul as ignoble and cowardly. David condemns the soldier to death for his lie. Praising Saul, David remembers him as patriot, as champion of his people: "The beauty of Israel is slain upon high places: how are the mighty fallen! . . . Ye daughters of Israel, weep over Saul, who clothed you in scarlet, with other delights, who put on ornaments of gold upon your apparel. How are the mighty fallen in the midst of battle" (II Samuel 1:19–27). David blesses those who bury him as hero and lays claim to the name of Saul to inspire his own leadership. In the *Critical Review* (August 1815), the reviewer also pointed to this same biblical source (especially II Samuel 1:22–26) with the suggestion that the song could be what David "chaunted . . . over the body of his friend Jonathan," the son of Saul who fell with his father on Mount Gilboa.

Nathan set "Thy Days are done" as a march, adding a four-part harmonization for the 1824–29 edition. Unfortunately, he allowed the military thrust to lapse into hymnal sentimentality. In exaggerating the elegiac portent, Nathan renders the meaning maudlin. He indicates in his notes, accurately enough, that it was Byron's purpose to invoke a general sense of tribute to "a fallen warrior, whose deeds remain a monument to the living." It has been suggested that this lyric addresses the death of Sir Peter Parker,[45] Byron's cousin, for whom he wrote the elegy appended to John Murray's edition of *Hebrew Melodies*. However, the celebration of "the fields he won, The freedom he restored!" would apply poorly to a naval officer whose service was gallant but always short of victory: He was advanced to captain after the battle of Trafalgar, a battle which had been fought and won by the time his ship arrived (October 1804). His attack on the *Pauline* in May 1812 may have been bold and brave, but he was repelled after his foretopmast was almost shot off. His career came to an end when he sailed his ship up the Chesapeake and led his crew of 134 in a rash attack on an American camp (August 1814). Forty of his men fell, including Parker himself who had been blasted with buckshot. The retreating crew carried their captain's body back to the ship. Byron's "Elegiac Stanzas" for his cousin gives due tribute to his bravery, but claims no victories. Unlike "Thy days are Done," the "Elegiac Stanzas" specifically address a naval career: "Sorrow's' purest sigh / O'er Ocean's heaving bosom sent." Not an elegy on Parker, neither was "Thy Days are done" a tribute to Napoleon, as many guessed, for Byron, at least according to Nathan, declared such a tribute would have been deserved only if Napoleon had fallen in battle and redeemed "his former intrepid career": "Napoleon would have ranked higher in future history, had he even, like your venerable ancestor Saul, on mount Gilboa, or like a second Cato, fallen on his sword and finished his mortal career at Waterloo" (*FP*, 39–40). Byron's hero, a "chosen son," sheds his blood as a martyr's sacrifice to save his people, in whom his blood will continue to flow. Although Nathan failed to realize it in his musical setting, this song is no funereal elegy but, like David's tribute, a martial call to persist in the fight:

Though thou art fall'n, while we are free
Thou shalt not taste of death!
The generous blood that flowed from thee
Disdained to sink beneath:
Within our veins its currents be,
Thy spirit on our breath!

The hero's death is not the subject of grief—"To weep would do thy glory wrong"; his name becomes, rather, a "battle word" to be taken up by the scattered survivors as they rally against their oppressors—"Thou shalt not be deplor'd."

A stirring military charge, "The Destruction of Sennacherib," has become a textbook example of "galloping anapests." Nathan's major task in setting this lyric was to create a melody capable of rising above the insistent anapestic rhythm. Byron's task, once he had turned to the account of the prophet Isaiah and King Hezekiah calling upon the Lord for protection against Sennacherib, king of Assyria, was to find an effective poetic mediation. Elsewhere he simply assumes identity, as Saul, or Eliphaz, or Herod, or Jephtha's Daughter. Here, rather than assuming the role of the prophet *pro persona,* Byron grandly absorbs the prophetic vision and tells of the destruction from an omniscient perspective. His sources gave him but a terse record of the event: "Then the angel of the Lord went forth, and smote in the camp of Assyrians an hundred fourscore and five thousand: and when they arose early in the morning, behold, they were all dead corpses" (Isaiah 37:36; II Kings 19:35).

There is no color, no spectacle, no pageantry. With the kind of visual opulence that would have delighted Cecil B. De Mille, Byron enriches the drama. Color and optical detail are crucial to Byron's rendition. In the opening stanza the poet shows us the Assyrian army "gleaming in purple and gold" and makes "the sheen of their spears" reflect dazzling pinpoints of light "like stars on the sea, / When the blue wave rolls nightly on deep Galilee." The similes informing the second stanza are temporal as well as visual: the army surrounds the city like a forest; as the sun sets, their banners are like the green leaves of summer; when it rises, the forest has been blasted by autumnal frost and the leaves lie "wither'd and strown." Nathan reproduces the turn from summer joy to autumn blast in the piano accompaniment. The third stanza attenuates the details of the biblical text by following the angel as it breathes death upon each soldier. The blasting of the forest leaves is reenacted as the deadly chill blights "the eyes of the sleepers." Stanzas four and five

"Jephtha's Daughter," a steel-plate engraving in William Finden's *Beauties of Byron; or, Portraits of the Principal Female Characters in Lord Byron's Poems,* London: Charles Tilt, undated. (Courtesy of Special Collections Room, Swilley Library, Mercer University in Atlanta)

offer close-up views of the dead: the battle steed lies with flared nostrils, the turf flecked white with "the foam of his gasping" like "the spray of the rock-beating surf" (a line that recalls "the blue wave . . . on deep Galilee"); the rider, too, lies "distorted and pale," his brow beaded in sweat much like the turf spattered with horse spittle. The biblical text describes Sennacherib retreating defeated to Ninevah. Byron, in his final stanza, emphasizes instead the triumph of Judaism as "the idols are broke in the temple of Baal." His concluding simile exercises once more the visual and temporal: the pomp and might of the pagans "melted like snow in the glance of the Lord."

"Little need be said of Byron's lyrics," Ian Jack asserted in his volume for the *Oxford History of English Literature*.[46] He was pleased enough to rank "the mastery of 'She Walks in Beauty'" alongside "the Caroline masters of lyric," but "Jephtha's Daughter" he judged "a resounding failure" and was content to quote the opening lines as sufficient proof:

Since our Country, our God—Oh, my Sire!
Demand that thy Daughter expire;
Since thy triumph was bought by thy vow—
Strike the bosom that's bared for thee now!

What qualities here contribute to "resounding failure"? Is it the daughter's controlled rational response to an awkward ethical situation which requires that she be sacrificed in order to uphold her father's honor? Or is it something inherent in the language, the syntax, in the rhythm presumed essential to the lyric? One critic, Josiah Condor, objected to the violation of taste "in attempting to accommodate subjects selected from the Hebrew Scriptures to the light measures of a love song" (*Eclectic Review,* July 1815). Another critic, William Roberts, considered "Jephtha's Daughter" the "unhappiest" performance in the collection: "The sentiments are out-done in deteriority by the metre, which is a sort of jumping anapaest, that would have suited the circumstances of the unhappy maid much better when she came out with timbrels and dances to meet her father, than when she was invoking the performance of his vow" (*British Review,* August 1815). Admittedly, the opening syllable of lines 1, 3, and 4 (2 opens with an iamb) carries a stress that weighs heavily on the anapestic cadence. Too, the pauses in the first line further disrupt the stride of anapests. Perhaps these "jumping anapests" are not anapests at all. Byron scarcely instills confidence in his skills of prosody when he says of *The Siege of Corinth* that a "great part . . . is in (I think) what the learned call Anapests (though I am not sure, being heinously forgetful of my metres & my 'Gradus')" (to John Murray, 20 February 1816). Before we let the critics or the poet himself convince us that he was clumsy when he tried to control anapestic rhythm, let us recall once more the irresistible "ta-ta-tum, ta-ta-tum" in "The Destruction of Sennacherib." The peculiar cadence of "Jephtha's Daughter" was created after Byron listened to Nathan playing what may have been the *Shir Hashirim,* and the Daughter's voice is carefully modulated to the rhythms of Nathan's proffered melody.

In urging her father to fulfill his promise, the daughter emphasizes her proud acceptance of fate, not as a duty but as a joy. There is no fear or despair in her words. The need to "bewail upon the mountains" has past. As she states in the second stanza, "the voice of my mourning is o'er." Byron has made her martyrdom at once beatific and triumphant, and Nathan has adapted his setting from cantillation traditionally associated with the Song of Songs. The moment that Byron has chosen to dramatize does not exist in the biblical account. Jephtha, the son of a harlot, has been driven forth from his father's house; he has survived as an outcast with a band of "vain men." When his people are threatened with war, they come to Jephtha and beg him to be their captain and fight their enemies. He is victorious, but he has "vowed a vow unto the Lord":

If thou shalt without fail deliver the children of Ammon into mine hands, then it shall be, that whatsoever cometh forth of the doors of my house to meet me, when I return in peace from the children of Ammon, shall surely be the Lord's, and I will offer it up for a burnt offering. (Judges 11:30–31)

The daughter, who comes out "with timbrels and with dances" to greet him, thus puts his honor on trial. The account in Judges describes her delaying the sacrifice for two months in order to "bewail her virginity upon the mountains." Upon her return we are told only that her father "did with her according to his vow." When Byron assumes the voice of the daughter, however, she has come down from the mountains to claim full share in her father's victory: "I have won the great battle for thee, / And my father and country are free."

Nathan thought this story might embarrass the attempt to celebrate the Jewish tradition. The tale of Jephtha and his daughter might be seen to prove precisely the kind of cruelty among the Jews that too many Christians were ready to believe. The reviewer for the *British Critic* (June 1815) preferred Thomas Morell's libretto for Handel's *Jephthah* (1752), in which the daughter's plea, "Ye sacred priests," fails to delay the cruel execution. It was such sad groveling and sadistic torment that both Nathan and Byron avoided. In his notes on the poem, Nathan repeats the rabbinical and talmudic interpretations which he shared with Byron and which prompted the poet's reply that, however the tale is interpreted, "my hands are not imbrued in her blood!" (*FP,* 8–15). Nathan emphasized that this tale, in spite of the parallel in Abraham and Isaac, was not peculiar to the Jews, but belonged to other cultures. Servius, in his commentary on the *Aeneid* (3.121), told how Idomeneus vowed to Poseidon that he would sacrifice the first thing that met him on his return. Nathan knew the story from Mozart's opera *Idomeneo* (1781). The folklorist will recognize two tales linked together: the beginning of the story belongs to the tale-types dealing with the fate of the abandoned child, "the exile returns and succeeds," the foundling hero (L 111.2) or the bastard hero (L 111.5); and the conclusion is a prime example of the tale-types concerning the child unwittingly promised (S 241), specifically the version stipulating the "first thing you meet" (types 425, 810).[47] Both tales involve what Bettelheim has labeled "separation anxiety," the fears of rejection or the insecurity when threatened by a parent's demands.[48] The two tales are linked by the vow that makes the separation of the daughter the condition for the bastard son's return. Too, both tales concern sexual maturation and sexual mores: Jephtha is born of a harlot and driven off when he comes to puberty; his daughter is sacrificed as a virgin, and much is made of her going off with her companions to bewail her virginity. In the words and music of "Jephtha's Daughter," Byron and Nathan have chosen to overcome the anxiety of separation with an emphasis on love and pride. The daughter participates in the very conditions that have influenced her father's fate; moreover, she can address him as an equal who also returns with valor from her exile: "Let my memory still be thy pride, / And forget not, I smiled as I died."

In drawing from the Book of Job, Byron ignored the narrative of the testing of Job and the disasters that befall him. He turned, rather, to the "wisdom" debate that takes up the central chapters. His text for "A Spirit Pass'd Before Me" is from Eliphaz's description of his vision (Job 4:13–21). Nathan's effuse oratorio setting provides grand amplitude for the voices of Eliphaz and his God. When William Blake illustrated the vision of Eliphaz, he made it clear that Eliphaz sees God in his own image. The question, "Shall a man be more pure than his maker?", contains multiple irony. Eliphaz has conjured the self-image of the God who then challenges him with the blasphemy of thinking himself godlike. Job, in Blake's illustration, is made to recognize in Eliphaz's vision not only the folly of his own presumption, but also Eliphaz's persistence in the error he pretends to denounce. Byron also treats the presumption of seeing God with irony. The manuscript of Byron's song "from Job" is written on the reverse side of "On Jordan's Banks." The voice of God that spoke to Moses from the burning bush (Exodus 3:2), descended on Mount Sinai in smoke and fire (Exodus 19:18), and refused to reveal his face because "there shall no man see me, and live" (Exodus 33:20) provides the source in "On Jordan's Banks" for Byron's lines. "Thy glory shrouded in its garb of fire: / Thyself—none living see and not expire!" In the Book of Job, the voice of God is heard from out of the whirlwind, scorning the vain claims of wisdom "that darkeneth counsel by words without knowledge" (Job 38–41). Yet Eliphaz asserts that God has appeared to him.

In his first stanza, Byron adapts the boast of Eliphaz: "I beheld / The face of Immortality unveiled— / Deep sleep came down on ev'ry eye but mine." Eliphaz does not appreciate the inadequacy of his vision. The "face" is obscured rather than revealed, for it remains "all formless." If this is a self-image, then there is a want of self-knowledge. Eliphaz suffers the human weakness of being more preoccupied with the body than with the spirit. In the moment of vision, he cannot escape the entanglements of his physical response: "Along my bones the creeping flesh did quake; / And my damp hair stiffened." In his second stanza, Byron echoes the voice of Eliphaz's God: "Is man more just than God? Is man more pure / Than he who deems even Seraphs insecure?" Although one reviewer objected that "the word *insecure* has no more business here than the nettle on the Monk's grave" (*Monthly Review,* September 1815), Byron has taken his "insecure" angels from the verse following, "Behold, he put no trust in his servants; and his angels he charged with folly." The words are like enough to those later spoken out of the whirlwind. Eliphaz, however, appropriates these words as his text for judging Job. When the voice of his vision concludes the indictment of human vanity, "they die, even without wisdom," he goes on to assume wisdom self-righteously in telling Job, "happy is the man whom God correcteth." Byron lets the vision close as an ironic self-indictment of the selfishly flesh-bound "Creatures of Clay" who pass their brief lives "Heedless and blind to Wisdom's wasted light!"

Byron based two poems on the Book of Daniel, "Vision of Belshazzar" (six stanzas) and "To Belshazzar" (three stanzas); both were composed at Seaham in February 1815. He apparently sent Nathan only the former, and the latter was not published by Murray until 1831. In the latter version, Byron speaks as Daniel castigating the king as vain voluptuary who trembles before the "graven words" still burning on the "glowing wall." It is too late to redeem his life from the wanton waste; too late, even, to recognize and renounce his vanity, "And learn like better men to die." The ultimate insult is not that he no longer deserves to live, but that he has become so degenerate and debased that he is unfit to die. In the version Nathan set with alternating melodies of oriental opulence and somber gravity, Byron assumes historical omniscience and Daniel speaks only the concluding stanza. The narrative begins with the king in his hall surrounded by splendor and sycophantic satraps. Like Sardanapalus, the effete king whose riches were amassed by the ruthless cunning and might of his predecessors, the self-indulgent Belshazzar sits amidst the booty that Nebuchadnezzar wrested from conquered Jerusalem when he destroyed the Temple and brought his captive slaves back to Babylon. Rather than risk shallow sentimentality in lamenting the exploitation of the Jews in captivity, Byron tersely observes the crude misuse of the "cups of gold" raped from the Temple: "Jehovah's vessels hold / The godless Heathen's wine" (Daniel 5:23) The second stanza describes the appearance of the hand, the third the fear of the monarch, the fourth the failure of the sages to read the mysterious words.

Jerome McGann notes that Daniel was an old man when he was called before Belshazzar to decipher the fatal text.[49]

Byron makes him still "a youth," the young Daniel who interpreted the dream of Nebuchadnezzar (in his alternate version, Byron has Daniel scorn a debilitated Belshazzar, son of Nebuchadnezzar, for adorning his "gray hairs" with "youth's garlands"). Daniel must neither decode nor grapple with the text; the "writing's truth" is simply and spontaneously revealed. The concluding stanzas of both versions present this truth. In the latter version, Daniel rebukes the king as "early in the balance weighed, / And ever light of word and worth." In the version sent to Nathan, Byron renders the line "He in the balance weighed, / Is light and worthless clay." Like Eliphaz and Saul, Belshazzar has clung too tightly to worldly means. But Eliphaz sought God, and Saul tried to redeem himself in death. For Belshazzar, who long since forfeited his soul, death only completes the corruption already infecting his vile flesh.

Byron also wrote two versions of Psalm 137, and he instructed Kinnaird to "take only one" for publication. Byron argued that "both are but different versions of the *same thought*."[50] Nathan, reluctant to lose any offering from Byron's pen, perceived differences and provided contrasting settings. Byron had marked his own preference for "In the Valley of Waters," and Nathan gave the words the melodic current of a motet. However, "We sate down," which Nathan set in a more passionate "sacred" mode, was selected for the 1816 edition. "Sacred" here does not mean solemn, for Nathan performed it with gusto, singing the words Byron had given the captive Jew so dramatically that the poet was amused: " 'Why, Nathan, you enter spiritedly into the oriental feeling: recollect, however, that although you *captivate,* you are no *captive*' " (FP, 45). When Nathan added the alternate version to the 1829 volume, he included this explanation:

When I submitted the MS. composition of this melody to Lord Byron, he seemed surprised, and observed that the subject had already been published. I pointed out the difference of style in my arrangement of them, and likewise how his Lordship had varied the present version. He remarked that in writing two he only wished me to make a selection, "but," added he, "I must confess I give preference to the latter, and since your music differs so widely from the former I see no reason why it should not also make its public appearance." (FP, 69)

If Nathan's memory here is accurate rather than merely convenient, "In the Valley of Waters" must have been the last song the composer presented to the poet. "We sate down" was not among the first twelve melodies published in April 1815; the statement that it "had already been published" could be made only after 18 April 1816, when the expanded edition appeared. Byron left London five days later.

As the contemporary reviews attest, Byron disrupted the generic expectations of his critics more in adapting from the Psalms than in any of his other uses of the "sacred model." Although he credited Byron as "superior to Moore . . . in the energy and strength of his style," the reviewer for the *Critical Review* (April 1816) objected to Byron's "profanation" and "burlesque" of the Scriptures. According to the critic in the *Monthly Review* (September 1815), Byron lost in his adaptation, "We sate down," all of the powerful and moving imagery of Psalm 137, "which has been so nobly versified by Tate." In expressing his regret that Byron has omitted the "affecting touches and the heart-rending pathos" of the original, this critic did not list among the missing beauties the concluding image of dashing "thy little ones against the stones." What had been echoed in Anglican hymnals of the gentle lamentation of singing "the Lord's song in a strange land," the reviewer wanted to hear repeated once more, but none of the bitter prayer for revenge and violence.

Of Byron's two versions, "We sate down" is the more diffuse in its defiance. When their enemies demand a song, the captives refuse. Byron describes the foe still bloody from battle, "in the hue of his slaughters." The pledge of resistance, "If I forget thee, O Jerusalem, let my right hand forget her cunning" (i.e., skill to play), Byron turns to a self-imposed curse against capitulation, "May this right hand be withered for ever / Ere it string our high harp for the foe." Byron told both Kinnaird and Nathan that he preferred the alternate version, "In the Valley of Waters." Here he turns from the first-person singular to the plural: "They called for the harp—but our blood they shall spill / Ere our right hands teach them one tone of their skill." He combines the original sense of "cunning" with a more pronounced declaration of resistance. In the opening stanza, he emphasizes the homeless deprivation of the captive Jews. In the second stanza, he reveals that a proud defiance triumphs over despair. In the third, he shows how faith informs an irrepressible spirit of freedom: "Our hands may be fettered—our tears still are free, / For our God and our glory—and, Sion!—Oh, thee."

HISTORY, SPECULATION, AND PROTO-ZIONISM

When we compare the ten poems based on the "sacred model" with these twelve poems that develop their thematic content from history, speculation, and proto-Zionism, we find no startling differences. With these poems Byron approaches the Bible just as often as he departed from it in those. Of course, he allows himself greater latitude and freedom, in the range of allusion, in the personal theologizing, and in the fervor of his polemics. He draws his history from non-biblical sources, as in "Herod's Lament for Mariamne" and "From the last Hill." He indulges an almost confessional speculation into the afterlife, as in "They say that Hope is Happiness," "Fame, Wisdom, Love, and Power were mine," "When Coldness wraps this suffering Clay," "If that High World," and "Bright be the place of thy soul." And he exercises a fervent proto-Zionism in "Oh! Weep for Those," "On Jordan's Banks," "The Harp the Monarch Minstrel Swept," "The Wild Gazelle," and "Were my Bosom as false." The portraits of Herod and the Penitent in "Fame, Wisdom" obviously should be hung in the gallery alongside those of Saul, Eliphaz, and Belshazzar. The graveside speculations, "Bright be the Place of thy Soul" and "When Coldness wraps this suffering Clay," address themes that we will find repeated, but bestowed upon the poet's "twilight" companion, in "Oh Snatch'd Away in Beauty's Bloom."

The principles of Byron's proto-Zionism are set forth simply and directly in his poems, and are informed by an uncomplicated sense of historical background. Zionism was not identified as an actual political movement until 1897, when the Basle Program defined the goals for legally establishing the Jewish people in Palestine. Nevertheless, the case for Zionism was clearly stated in the Bible: "the Lord thy God will bring thee into the Land which thy fathers possessed, and thou shalt possess it" (Deuteronomy 30:5). One kind of Zionism grew over the centuries with the desperate yearning to escape the ghetto. This smouldering Zionism was sometimes fanned into flame by opportune liberators, from David Reubeni in 1530 and Sabbatai Sebi in 1666, to Richard Brothers, "Prince of Hebrews," in 1793. Another kind of Zionism, encouraged by Christian Millenarians who were eager to send all the Jews back to the Holy Land, was nourished by the tenets of Richard Hurd and Joseph Priestley. Contrary to the efforts of Zionism, the Mendelssohnian movement aspired to full cultural integration of the Jew in Europe. Following the influence of Moses Mendelssohn's *Jerusalem* (1783), the *Haskalah* (Enlightenment) had spread to England, and the principles of educational emancipation were fostered by Solomon Lyon in the Anglo-Jewish school that Nathan attended. The Mendelssohnian idea was to coordinate talmudic discipline with broad intellectual training in the general European culture. But the Mendelssohnian *Maskilim* also promoted the "Science of Judaism," a thorough evaluation of the history of the Jewish people. The result was a new ethnic consciousness and national awareness. Although the Grand Sanhedrin convened by Napoleon in 1806 may have temporarily dampened the zeal of Zionist nationalism, the very concerns of post-revolutionary republicanism encouraged the expatriate Jew to pursue the cause of his own national freedom in the Holy Land.[51] The dilemma was twofold: he was bound to traditional rabbinical teaching, yet he was expected to know the issues current in society; he was to strive politically and spiritually for the return of his homeland, but he was to be a loyal subject of his adopted country. Encouraged by the *Maskilim* to seek a place in society, he was exposed more than ever to anti-Semitic prejudice. Not unlike the reception Nathan experienced from Kinnaird and Hobhouse.

"Oh! Weep for Those," the only poem among Byron's initial offering to Nathan that deliberately responded to the plan for Hebrew "national airs," drew psalmlike characteristics from Psalm 137 and other biblical sources. "In the Valley of Waters" developed a similar pattern: amidst the grief, fear, sadness of persecution, there swells a proud, stubborn defiance. But here Byron attempts to raise the intensity of the Zionist cause, to reclaim the desolate shrines and fulfill the dream of the homeland. In proclaiming the triumph over the wicked, David declared that the righteous "shall rejoice when he seeth the vengeance: he shall wash his feet in the blood of the wicked" (Psalm 58:10). Upon the overthrow of Tyre, Isaiah prophesies that the fallen will be neglected as a "harlot" but will then rise again: "Take an harp, go about the city, thou harlot that hast been forgotten; make sweet melody, sing many songs, that thou mayest be remembered" (Isaiah 23:16). In his second stanza, Byron lets the allusions smolder as insistent questions of determined protest: "And where shall Israel lave her bleeding feet? / And when shall Zion's songs again seem sweet?" Nathan enhanced the inherent march rhythm by setting it to a blessing chant. The allusions of the third stanza further complicate the irony: "The wild-dove hath her nest, the fox his cave, / Mankind their Country—Israel but the grave!" In spite of the parallelism which invites us to read "Israel" as metonymy for the Jews, Byron intends it as evanescent symbol, the lost as well as the future Zion. The grave as mere plot of ground, after all, belongs to all mankind and every country. Byron draws from the New Testament the words of Christ to those who would follow him: "The foxes have holes, and the birds of the air have nests; but the Son of man hath not where to lay his head. . . . Follow me; and let the dead bury the dead" (Matthew 8:20,22). Byron counters the negative resolution of the grave, not with the pretension that the salvation of the Jews lies in following Christ, but with the revelation that Christ himself had affirmed restless wandering as a part of the spiritual commitment.

"On Jordan's Banks," another pseudo psalm, was written on the reverse of Byron's song from Job. In that song, as we have seen, Eliphaz claimed to see God. And in this one we are reminded that "none living see and not expire!" Although the land has been usurped by the "Baal-adorers," it is God's country and the intruders trespass where the divine "thunders sleep." The second stanza points emphatically to Mount Sinai where "the Lord descended . . . in fire" and "the people saw the thunderings and lightnings" (Exodus 19:18, 20:18). The third stanza calls upon God, "to whom vengeance belongeth," once again to show himself (Psalm 94) and to send forth out of his thunders the lightning to scatter and destroy (Psalm 144): "in the lightning let thy glance appear!" The concluding lines borrow from the Psalms the recurrent lament, "O Lord, How long?" (As in Psalms 4, 6, 13, 35, 74, 89, 90, 94).

"The Harp the Monarch Minstrel Swept" tells two stories: one similar to Moore's "The Harp that once, thro' Tara's halls," the other more like Dryden's "Song for St. Cecilia's Day." One relates music to the past glory of the nation, the other identifies music with divine harmony. David, "the Monarch Minstrel," is at once "The King of men, the loved of Heaven." After his music is "hallowed" by the heartfelt response of heaven, it works a divine power upon men: "It gave them virtues not their own." David brought the Ark of the Covenant into the center of the new nation and his music glorified its power: "David's Lyre grew mightier than his throne!" In the third stanza, Byron relates the song of the harp: "It told the triumphs of our King, / It wafted glory to our God." Nathan tells us that Byron originally gave him a draft that terminated with this stanza. Nathan asked for another stanza "to help out the melody," for he had a martial tune and wanted to hold the pomp and majesty in a strophic balance. Byron protested, "'Why I have sent you to Heaven—it would be difficult to go further.'" After a few moments, the poet exclaimed, "'Here, Nathan, I have brought you down again,' and immediately presented me the beautiful and sublime lines which conclude the melody" (*FP,* 33). This last stanza declares that, though the harp is silent, devotion and love "Still bid the bursting spirit soar / To sounds that seem as from above."

"The Wild Gazelle," in Nathan's setting, lacks the second stanza. Perhaps Nathan omitted it from the vocal part because the poet's pause to flirt with "Judah's statelier maids" seemed too stark a distraction from the emotional tone of the other stanzas. Byron begins with the graceful beauty of the gazelle, exulting and bounding over the "holy ground." The point, of course, is that the wild animal still enjoys the provenance that has been denied to Judah's sons and daughters. Byron holds that point in abeyance, only to bring it forth more powerfully in his conclusion. After delighting in the "airy step and glorious eye" of the gazelle, he goes on, in the second stanza, to appraise those maidens whom he finds as nimble as the wild gazelle yet with "an eye more bright." But these fair inhabitants are gone. The third stanza describes the palm "More blest . . . / Than Israel's scattered race." The palm is rooted to the soil and "cannot quit its place of birth." Nathan has let his melody appropriately exult and bound with the gazelle, and sway with the palm's "solitary grace"; he then darkens to a dirge to set Byron's grim conclusion: "But we must wander witheringly, / In other lands to die." Not only bereft of their natural home, they must witness their land occupied by false intruders, while "Mockery sits on Salem's throne."

"Were my Bosom as false," with Nathan's original setting of 1815, continued to be popular, among the most-often sung of the *Hebrew Melodies.* In spite of its vigorous challenge to Christian prejudice, this song was received as amatory. Indeed, in *The Universal Songster* it is listed among the love songs.[52] Nathan's original setting seems to have caused the general misinterpretation of the song's meaning. No doubt he intended to correct the response when he replaced his lighthearted tones with gloomy ones in 1829. This does not mean, however, that his original setting was "wrong." The light lilt which carries the defiant message suits well that blithe and mocking Byronic persona who turns the accusations of "false" back upon his accusers. First, he points out that if he were "false," he need only convert from Jew to Christian "to efface / The curse which, thou say'st, is the crime of my race." In the second stanza, he delivers cutting irony with seeming ingratiation: "If the bad never triumph, then God is with thee! / If the slave only sin, thou art spotless and free!" A voice that had mastered such smiling scorn might sing Nathan's first version very effectively. In spite of its irony, the song, a sort of love song after all, clearly aims at benevolent reconciliation of the exiled Jew and his Christian host. In the last stanza, he humbly surrenders "my heart and my hope" to the hand of God, and leaves in the hand of his host "The land and the life which for him I resign."

"From the last Hill" provides an eyewitness report "On the Day of the Destruction of Jerusalem by Titus." The day was 8 September A.D. 70. Byron derives his story from Josephus, *Wars of the Jews* (Book VI, chs. viii–ix; Book VII, ch. v).[53] Josephus, who had earlier been captured and liberated by Vespasian, now reports the attack of Titus against the rebel "tyrants" John and Simon. Although he condemns the rebellion and argues in behalf of Roman allegiance, Josephus does not fail to reveal the brutality of the Romans when they broke in upon the city already weakened by famine. Pillage and slaughter belong to the arts of war, yet Josephus could scarcely sustain his objectivity in describing the bloody horror within the fallen city. For this lyric, Byron assumes his role as one of the captives, "with fast-fettered hands that made vengeance in vain." Even in bondage, he curses the Roman triumph. Nathan has tempered the defiance by providing a hymnal setting to the captive's last look at his lost home. He recalls, in the third stanza, seeing "many an eve" of sunset glory descending on the city. In the fourth stanza, as the last "twilight beam" glares upon the ruins, he wishes "that the lightning had glared in its stead, / And the thunderbolt burst on the conqueror's head!" Such, in "On Jordan's Banks," was the wish of that witness to the pagans within the Temple on whom he would rouse the lightning from God's eye of thunder. The final stanza reaffirms Jewish faith in resistance to the pagan captivity: "And scattered and scorned as thy people may be, / Our worship, oh Father! is only for thee."

"Herod's Lament for Mariamne" is a reflection on jealous passion, the selfish possessiveness that drives man to destroy what he most desires. The *Hebrew Melodies* offer several portraits of men tormented because they have succumbed to selfish passions: Saul sees Samuel; Belshazzar sees the handwriting on the wall; Eliphaz sees the formless face of immortality; Jephtha sees his Daughter baring her bosom for sacrifice; and Herod sees himself damned to desolation, bereft of his "murdered love." The source for the story is Josephus, *Antiquities of the Jews* (Book XV, ch. vii), although Byron probably drew from Voltaire's tragedy, *Mariamne* (1725). Mariamne, Josephus wrote, "treated her husband

Introduction / 25

imperiously enough, because she saw he was so fond of her as to be enslaved of her." She had a "saucy manner," openly defied Herod's sister, Salome, and often reproached her husband for murdering her grandfather and brother. One hot noon, he called for her, but she denied his desires and "refused to lie down by him." Observing Herod's anger, Salome bribed his cupbearer to say that Mariamne had requested him to prepare a love potion. Salome's stratagem succeeded in stirring the king to such a jealous rage that he commanded Mariamne's execution. After her death, "his love to Mariamne seemed to seize him in such a peculiar manner, as looked like the divine vengeance upon him for taking away her life, and he would frequently call for her, and frequently lament her in a most indecent manner." It is Herod's "indecent manner," his "dark heart . . . vainly craving," that Byron chooses for this lyric, a song of madness far more morbid than that sung by Saul in "My Soul is Dark." Like Manfred conjuring Astarte, Herod longs for her forgiveness: "Ah, could'st thou—thou would'st pardon now, / Though heaven were to my prayer unheeding." He condemns his court for daring to "Obey my phrensy's jealous raving," and he sees suspended over his own head, like the sword of Damocles, "the sword that smote her." Herod resigns himself, without Manfred's defiance, to the hell of mind's making and the doom of "this bosom's desolation."

In "'All is Vanity, saith the Preacher'" ("Fame, Wisdom, Love, and Power were mine"), Byron models his moral after Ecclesiastes. Like Herod and Belshazzar, the speaker has lavished in fleshly pleasures: "My goblets blushed from every vine, / And lovely forms caressed me." Now he looks back on his life for the one moment that "would lure him to live over." No such ecstasy tempts: he recalls "no hour / Of pleasure unembittered," no show of power "That galled not while it glittered." He has rejected the world of the flesh but still can find no comfort for the spirit. He fears not the "serpent of the field," which by "spells, is won from harming," but the unseen serpent "which coils around the heart." In "Dejection: An Ode," Coleridge sought to abjure the "viper thoughts, that coil around my mind." Just as insidious is this serpent "which coils around the heart," for no charm, nor wisdom, nor music "can lure it." The word "lure" here identifies the kinship of the serpent of the mind with the unfound temptation of the past. In the wisdom of Ecclesiastes, we are warned "He that diggeth a pit shall fall into it; and whoso breaketh a hedge, a serpent shall bite him. . . . Surely the serpent will bite without enchantment" (10:8, 11). Byron's serpent preys upon "Creatures of Clay" who have prized the experience of sensual delight yet found it empty: "it stings for evermore / The soul that must endure it."

"They say that Hope is Happiness" deserves a place among the deft and ingenious exercises in paradox. Byron turns this vicious circle on the axis of temporal consciousness. He pretends to counter the claim "that Hope is Happiness" with the declaration that "Love must prize the past" and "mem'ry wakes the thoughts that bless." Not hope for the future, then, but the memory of the past offers the true blessing. Memory, however, "loves the most" the early "hope to be"; indeed, memory is principally the repository of former hopes, "adored and lost." Each hope, Byron wrote to Moore, appears as a painted maiden only to be exposed as a "hollow-cheeked harlot" (28 October 1815).[54] The third stanza is the cry within this vicious circle, "Alas! it is delusion all— / The future cheats us from afar." Byron offers still another turn to this paradox. The worst is not that hope fails to fulfill memory, but that the delusions of the past and the future leave us unable to accept the present: "Nor can we be what we recall, / Nor dare we think on what we are."

The play of paradox obviously frustrated Kinnaird. By sending Byron a copy of the Rev. Edward Smedley's *Saul* (1814) and *Jephtha* (1815), he may deserve some credit for promoting, at least indirectly, the inclusion of these subjects on the "sacred model." On the other hand, he might also be held responsible for almost destroying "They say that Hope is Happiness," which Byron had "consigned to the flames" in response to Kinnaird's "officious" remarks on supposed "demerits." Nathan, however, had already set the piece to music, and Byron subsequently granted his appeal to resurrect "the *sacrifice,*" as "a *peace offering*" rather than as "a *burnt offering,*" and to preserve it among the *Melodies* (FP, 71).

"When Coldness wraps this suffering Clay" questions not whether but "whither" the mind passes into eternity. Byron does not doubt the immortality of mind; rather, he asks where consciousness abides after it "leaves its darkened dust behind." The mind, he speculates, must endure as "A thing of eyes," gazing throughout "the realms of space," beholding the All. He thus defines the soul as "unembodied" thought still capable of visual perception, "A thought unseen, but seeing all." He repeats this definition in *Childe Harold,* III, when he argues that "the mind shall be all free / From what it hates in this degraded form," and shall participate in nature as "bodiless thought" and "Feel all I see, less dazzling, but more warm" (11. 698–706).[55] With echoes from Paul's hymn to love, "For now we see through a glass, darkly; but then face to face" (I Corinthians 13:12), Byron claims an emancipation of memory as well as perception for the all-beholding-mind:

All, all in earth, or skies displayed,
Shall it survey, shall it recall:
Each fainter trace that memory holds
So darkly of departed years,
In one broad glance the soul beholds,
And all, that was, at once appears.

Not only the personal memory is revealed to the bodiless eye, all time and all space open up to its perception—the past ("Its eye shall roll through chaos back") as well as the future ("Its glance dilate o'er all to be"). The opening question, "whither strays the immortal mind?", is answered in the closing stanza with the absolute transcendence of mind permeating every dimension of the universe, "O'er all, through all, its thought shall fly." Identity, however, has been lost, left behind with the "suffering clay." The "thing of eyes" is now I-less, "A nameless and eternal thing," no longer bound by such selfish constraint as limited the mortally blighted vision of Eliphaz or Saul.

Forever penetrating the All may be a prolonged love-act of selfless bliss. Byron, however, also posits an eternity of self-bound torment. As dwelling place of the soul and as the "eternal thing" surviving this "suffering clay," the eye may behold nothing more than its own damned being, its own past deeds forever reenacted. Echoing Satan (*Paradise Lost*, I, 254–255), Manfred tells the demons who come to fetch him that the mind "makes itself / Requital for its good and evil thoughts." In explaining the mind's mode of perception, Manfred declares that it sees with "innate sense." Instead of deriving "colour from the fleeting things without," the mind "is absorbed in sufferance or in joy, / Born from the knowledge of its own desert" (III, iv, 129–136). In *The Bride of Abydos*, Byron wrote of Zuleika "that eye was in itself a Soul," and of Selim "the soul of that eye" flashed forth like lightning from a black cloud (I, 181, 338). When he rides forth to avenge "lost Leila," the Giaour searches with an "evil eye," and when he confronts his enemy, Hassan declares "I know him by his evil eye" (*The Giaour*, I, 196, 612). In his notes to the poem, Byron identified the "evil eye" as "a common superstition in the Levant, and of which the imaginary effects are yet very singular on those who conceive themselves effected."

The *malocchio* or *böser Blick* had a special place in Hebraic wisdom, for Solomon had warned, "He that hasteth to be rich hath an evil eye" and "Eat thou not the bread of him that hath an evil eye" (Proverbs 23:6, 28:22). Nathan narrated several "curious anecdotes recorded in Hebrew" relative to the evil eye and the wisdom of the Cabala. And he gave Byron a Hebrew charm for warding off the "evil eye" which had "been handed down from father to son, since the building of the first temple" (*FP*, 120–121). Byron, however, needed no prompting from Nathan, for he repeatedly describes a power glaring from the eye of judgment. When Samuel arose at the summons of the Witch of Endor, he stared upon Saul and "Death stood all glassy in his fixed eye." The eye that glances "in the lightning," in "On Jordan's Banks," blasts "from his shivered hand the oppressor's spear." The eyes that roll and dilate throughout eternity, in "When Coldness wraps this suffering Clay," survey the cosmos much as Cain,

And yet I have approach'd that sun, and seen
Worlds which he once shone on, and never more
Shall light; and worlds he never lit . . .
I had beheld the immemorial works
Of endless beings; skirr'd extinguish'd worlds;
And, gazing on eternity, methought
I had borrow'd more by a few drops of ages
From its immensity . . . (III, i, 56–67)

Unlike the "thing of eyes" which unites with that immensity, however, Cain remains an estranged looker-on. Byron knew the vision of godless immortality as Madame de Staël had told it, translating from Jean Paul's "Rede des todten Christus," in *De l'Allemagne* (published by John Murray, October 1813). The resurrected Christ searches the heavens for the eye of God but finds only a vast empty eye socket. Not even Cain, in his grim apostasy, is made to look upon an eyeless, godless universe. Like Eliphaz, Cain conjures his own terrific image of God, a God who first flatters our mortal dust "with glimpses of / . . . Immortality" and then scorns us with reminders of "the *nothing* which we are" (III, i, 70–74).

"If that High World," wrote the critic for the *Christian Observer* (August 1815), avoids the mistake of giving to the soul become "all eye" the divine attributes of "omnipresence and omnipotence"; however, it makes the opposite mistake of granting the soul too little. Because Byron would not affirm, with Eliphaz, a confrontation with God, the critic found the sentiment of the first stanza "incomplete," the second stanza "obscure." Nathan, who expressed his concern that the opening "If" might invite the ready charge of Byron's atheism (*FP*, 5–6), chose to accentuate the positive with a setting adapted from the Kaddish. Although sung as a mourner's prayer, the Kaddish is a hymn praising God. Byron again speculates upon a soul that keeps its love and persists as sight, "The eye the same, except in tears." If these conditions be granted, "How welcome those untrodden spheres." Only joy would be exposed to the soul's eye, and "all fears / Lost in thy light—Eternity." The second stanza, "It must be so," is as strong an affirmation of faith as Byron ever uttered in his poetry. He argues that we "tremble on the brink" not because we fear to sacrifice the self but because we are unready to embrace the other. Thus we "cling to Being's severing link" when we should, instead, anticipate an immortal merging of "soul in soul."

In "Bright be the Place of thy Soul," Byron ponders once again "whither" the soul. The eye may be the place of the soul, but here it is promised that the loveliest of souls ever to "burst from its mortal control" will henceforth shine "In the orbs of the blessed." The first stanza thus describes the transcendent soul assuming divine radiance. The second stanza expresses the wish that the grave therefore be arrayed in appropriate visual splendor: "its verdure like emeralds" planted with evergreens and springing flowers, and no dark cypress nor yew. The living should celebrate rather than mourn the blessed dead. Darkness must yield to light. "There should not be shadow of gloom, / In aught that reminds us of thee."

Apparently Nathan's light tenor voice stirred Byron's

memory of John Edleston, the choirboy at Trinity Chapel.⁵⁶ Describing two years of "almost constant" intimacy with Edleston at Cambridge, Byron wrote: "his *voice* first attracted my notice, his *countenance* fixed it, & his *manners* attached me to him forever" (to Elizabeth Pigot, 30 June 1807). On learning of Edleston's death in 1811, he recorded his grief in "Epistle to a Friend," "To Thyrza," and "Away, away, ye notes of woe." The third of these poems was provoked by "hearing a song of former days" and recalling "The voice that made those sounds more sweet" (to Francis Hodgson, 8 Dec 1811). "Bright be the Place of thy Soul" also indulges the memory of Thyrza. When Nathan described his performing the song at Byron's request in the Green Room of Drury Lane, he explained that it was "a song his Lordship had only that morning written for me, impromptu." Shortly after the performance in the Green Room, Leigh Hunt printed the poem in the *Examiner* (11 June 1815) and Nathan issued it with his music as a song sheet. The song was not included in the 1816 edition, nor did Nathan add it to the 1829 volume. Murray began printing it with the *Hebrew Melodies* in 1819. Nathan, however, put it aside. Even in his *Fugitive Pieces* (1829), he places the poem in the biographical "Reminiscences" (*FP*, 114), rather than among the "entire new edition of the Hebrew Melodies" (*FP*, 1–81). Because it appeared only as a song sheet, the musical setting of "Bright be the Place of thy Soul" is an extreme rarity in the already rare collection.

THE TWILIGHT MUSE

"She Walks in Beauty" is the perfect invocation to the Muse of these melodies, a muse of twilight, in exile from the "gaudy day" and treading the shadowy boundaries of night. To be sure, Byron had seen her incarnate. Whatever motives had prompted Anne Wilmot to attend the ball while still in mourning, moreover to decorate her black mourning gown with spangles, she could have little conceived how her appearance would thus excite the poet's image of perfect liminal poise, "One shade the more, one ray the less, / Had half impair'd the nameless grace." Despite the daring of her smiles and blushes, Byron insists that she keeps "a mind at peace with all below." Among other bodily parts "below" her mind, her heart must certainly be counted, and its love is "innocent." She not only walks in beauty, she coquettishly limns the surrounding darkness. Yet she was not the sole model of a muse capable of sustaining in felicitous balance "all that's best of dark and bright."

Byron described other serene beauties who glide the edge of night. The song sequence is not only introduced by such a twilight muse; Byron leads her graveside in "Oh Snatch'd Away" and reveals the chiaroscuro of her emotions in "I saw thee Weep." She is made to reappear again in the closing song of the 1815 edition, "It is the Hour" (song 12), and, at the close of the 1816 edition, in "Francisca" (song 23) and "Sun of the Sleepless!" (song 24). Byron provided seven of these twilight études on the shadowy boundaries of love and life, but Nathan withheld until after the poet's death "I Speak Not—I Trace Not," the contradictory song of defiance and love, abjuring and conjuring, parting and uniting.

"It is the Hour," fourteen lines of iambic tetrameter, has a sonnetlike structure, an ABABCC sestet followed by an octave of four couplets. The opening, titular line defines time in transition, that hour in which "twilight melts . . . away" and day turns to night. Byron charges the "hour" with sensually rich yet secretive anticipation. The contrasts of intimacy and isolation are provided in the opening sestet: "lovers' vows" are "whispered," yet only the music of "winds and waters" plays "to the lonely ear." In the octave the contrasts continue in a parallel series: the togetherness of flowers touched by the dews and the stars met in the sky vs. the solitary wave darkening to a "deeper blue" and the desolate leaf turning a "browner hue." The stars and flowers are placed within a natural order of intimate interpenetration; the wave and leaf are isolated, their gloom wrought within. The concluding four lines achieve a paradoxical balance at the edge of night's darker, deeper distances. In the very moment of transition, Byron evokes, not the "darkness visible" of Milton's Hell, but "that clear obscure, / So softly dark—and darkly pure, / That follows the decline of day." The paradoxical union of clarity and obscurity prompts the eyes to peer into the invitingly penetrable, still virginally unpenetrated depth of soft, pure darkness. This is the moment before the dews wet the flowers, before the stars meet in the sky, yet after the somber change of wave and leaf. The hour of the "nightingale's high note" is the hour of transition and change, of loneliness and intimacy, "As twilight melts beneath the moon away."

Nathan altered Byron's sestet-octave structure into two strophic octaves. By including the lines on the flowers and stars (7–8), he has his first strophe; by repeating the lines on the "clear obscure" (11–12), he has provided for eight lines in the second strophe. The repetition succeeds in emphasizing the paradoxical balance that links this poem to the thematic concerns introduced in "She Walks in Beauty."

When John Murray found this same lyric as the opening stanza of *Parisina*, he deleted it from subsequent editions of the *Hebrew Melodies*. Murray had never included "Francisca," which became the second stanza of *Parisina*. Byron had probably included both of these among the poems he first gave to Nathan to satisfy Kinnaird's plea. It has been suggested that "Francisca" was an errant stanza composed while Byron was creating the character of Francesca for *The Siege of Corinth*. In any case, it is not likely that Byron had originally conceived of these poems as belonging to his tale of incestuous love. Even if he was aware that Byron had thus made these poems introduce an illicit tryst between Parisina and her husband's handsome bastard son, Nathan did not change his mind about their thematic suitability to the *Hebrew Melodies*. Nathan had already used "It is the Hour" to close the first sequence of twelve songs. His second sequence, published two months after *Parisina*, contains ten of the eleven songs Byron wrote for him, in spite of the disagreement over Murray's right to the poetry, during January and February. This second series Nathan chose to conclude with "Francisca" followed by "Sun of the Sleepless!," another of the very first poems he had received from Byron, but one that again separates the lovers. "Francisca" moves from hopeful anticipation to union. "Sun of the Sleepless!" leaves the disconsolate lover alone and longing.

Although "Francisca" continues, or rather consummates, the evocations of "It is the Hour" (the lines that it follows in *Parisina*), Nathan has conceived this song as a companion to "She Walks in Beauty," for here is another muse who "walks in the shadow of night," delicately sustaining her balance along the boundary between light and dark; the line she treads may be invisible, but a dangerous trespass attends her slightest misstep. The images of "It is the Hour" are repeated but denied: Francisca has entered the darkened garden "not to gaze on the heavenly light," "not for the sake of its blowing flower," "not for the nightingale," but perhaps for whisperings of "lovers' vows." The deepening colors within the solitary wave and leaf are mirrored in her transformation: "her cheek grows pale—and her heart beats quick. / There whispers a voice thro' the rustling leaves, / And her blush returns." "It is the Hour" anticipates, even through the final line, the moment in which "twilight melts beneath the moon away." In the closing line of "Francisca," the moment is no longer anticipated: "'Tis past—her Lover's at her feet."

Following the secret tryst uniting Francisca and her lover, the final song, "Sun of the Sleepless!," has the lover lament his separation. Nathan, with the naive persistence he often assumed—at least in his recorded dialogues—asked Lord Byron "whether the *moon* or the *evening star*, both receiving their light from the *sun*," should be identified as the "melancholy star." Byron replied that Nathan's "*star gazing*" had left him "in the *clouds*," and that he should consult the Astronomer Royal for his answer. Nathan, however, had already consulted his cantorial sources to support musically his own identification of the distant star with the prophecy of Balaam: "there shall come a Star out of Jacob, and a Sceptre shall rise out of Israel, and shall smite the corners of Moab, and destroy all the children of Sheth" (Numbers 24:17). For the Jews, this text defined the Star of David, that sign that once led the triumph over the Moabites and would continue to shield valiant Israel. This same text, of course, was read as a prophecy of the Star of Bethlehem and the coming of the Messiah, as affirmed by Christ: "I am the root and offspring of David, and the bright and morning star" (Revelation 22:17). The song of the estranged lover became for Nathan a Hebrew melody of the long, lonely vigil, waiting for "the light of other days" to shine again. Even without emphasizing the equation of the "Sun of the Sleepless" with the Star of David, or whatever the Astronomer Royal might advise, Nathan found thematic relevance for the *Hebrew Melodies* in the liminal play of light in darkness that dominated the imagery of this song as well as several of the other lyrics Byron had included in his first offering. To the "Sleepless" tribe who watch the "melancholy star," its "tearful beam glows tremulously far." Byron indulges no "pathetic fallacy." The "melancholy star" has a venerable place in the macrocosm: Saturn, or Rimmon the "High Star" of Damascus, was the star identified in astrological and cabalistic lore as influencing the body's melancholera. The star casts a "tearful beam" because such refraction is produced only as the light strikes the fluid bathing the eye, "tremulously far" but as near as tears. Again evoking the "clear obscure," Byron declares that the light can only reveal but not dispel the reigning darkness. He closes the first quatrain with the simile, "How like thou art to joy remembered well," which he further extends in the second quatrain. The "Sun of the Sleepless" becomes, then, "the light of other days," which "gleams" from the past and "shines" without warmth, without power. "Sorrow" now assumes the place of the "Sleepless" in holding the vigil, while the "night-beam" continues to cast its light in darkness, "Distinct, but distant—clear—but, oh how cold!"

"Oh! snatch'd Away in Beauty's Bloom," like "Bright be the Place of thy Soul," may also recollect the death of John Edleston. That poem calls for the transformation of the grave into springtime vitality to celebrate the radiant glory of the transcendent soul. This poem similarly decorates the grave with roses. While the poet here allows the "tender gloom" of the "wild cypress," he confesses the inappropriateness of grief. Yet in conjuring the fond but futile weeping of an allegorical Sorrow, the poet transfers the weeping to his companion who hears the tale. At the very time she agreed to accept his suit of marriage, Byron gave this poem to Annabella (November 1814). Did he tell her of his love for Thyrza? Did she share the tears of the listening companion in the poem? "And thou—who tell'st me to forget, / Thy looks are wan, thine eyes are wet." Upon his return from Seaham to London at the end of the month, Byron presented the poem to Nathan to be set with the *Hebrew Melodies*. When Nathan wanted to know "in what manner they might refer to any scriptural subject," Byron replied that "every mind must make its own reference." An added gloss to the poem is Byron's reflection, also recorded by Nathan, that the last surviving vestige of the dead is the image fondly indulged by the living.

Although he teases with sorrow in "Oh! Snatch'd Away," the poet does not attempt in "I saw thee Weep" to urge the tears of his companion. Rather, he delights equally in her weeping and in her smiling as moments that portray the chiaroscuro complexity of her beauty. Byron celebrates the dusk and dawn twilight that plays in "that eye of blue." The "violet dropping dew" and "the sapphire's blaze," contradictory images of darkness and light, become visually apt images for the emotional contraries in these revealing eyes. The eyes not only reflect the inner feelings, their "living rays" outshine the competing lights of day. To this poetic commonplace Byron adds attentive detail, explaining how, amidst "the shade of coming eve," these eyes absorb the fading light just "As clouds from yonder sun receive / A deep and mellow dye." The image recalls, from "She Walks in Beauty," the eyes "Thus mellowed to that tender light." Their twilight glimmer penetrates "the moodiest mind" and "leaves a glow behind / That lightens o'er the heart." Just as the immortal mind persists as "a thing of eyes" in "When Coldness wraps this suffering Clay," the mind of the living also finds its chief outlet in the eyes. Nathan noted that this concern with the "fine distinction of opposite feelings" revealed in the eyes was typical of the often repeated "dissertation on the organ of sight" in which the poet was "always eulogizing the characteristic expression of the eye." Climaxing this particular eulogy, Byron declared that he "put more faith in the language" of the eyes than in "all the falacious rules of Lavater, Gall, or Spurzheim" (FP, 35).

"I Speak Not—I Trace Not—I Breathe Not thy name" is a song of forbidden love. Language is made to belie its own activity: in speaking the unspeakable, the poet begins with the paradoxical "I speak not." The guilt arises not from the act but from the utterance: "There is grief in the sound." Shifting to the subjunctive ("there were guilt in the fame"), he predicts the consequences: should that word be gossiped forth, the public would speak it as moral trespass. The lovers' fate, however, resides apart from society's pronouncement of guilt. Byron affirms an intimacy that risks, yet scorns the risk—that accepts only the reward or the reproof of the relationship. Just as the lovers speak the unspeakable, they conjure in the very act of abjuring: "We repent—we abjure—we will break from our chain: / We must part—we must fly to—unite it again." The concern with salvation, to be granted by the forbidden lover not by church or society, was a turn later appropriated for Manfred's promise to Astarte to "bear / This punishment for both," to die that she might be blessed (II, iv, 124–126). The cancelled lines, "And thine is that love which I will not forego, / Though the price which I pay be Eternity's woe," boldly defy damnation. The concluding stanza proclaims the independence of the lovers, untouched by the prejudice that banishes them. Even those who condemn are awed by their strength to endure, oblivious to condemnation: "And the heartless may wonder at all we resign, / Thy lip shall reply not to them—but to mine." Nathan recalled playing this "scherzando discrezione" as well as "Herod's Lament for Mariamne" for Leigh Hunt on the morning before Byron left London. Too intimate, too defiant a declaration of love beyond the pale, this celebration of Byron's twilight muse would obviously further fuel the already raging scandal. Byron imposed the condition that the song, if published, should be dated two years prior to his marriage. When it was included in the 1829 volume, Nathan told this story, quoting Byron's insistence that he publish the song for the music's sake: "'I am too great an admirer of your music to suffer a single *phrase* of it be lost'" (FP, 66).

The Character of Nathan's Settings

We know that Nathan used authentic musical materials of his age, and that Byron responded to those materials, putting "Jewishness" into his lyrics in a way that surprised Nathan. But what, finally, are we to make of the music on its own merits and in relation to the words? And when we listen to the sequence of individual pieces, what patterns, if any, do we discover in the cycle of *Hebrew Melodies* as a whole?

One hears in Nathan's music, where it occurs for the first time, the great impact Byron was to have in the music of the nineteenth century. One thinks, of course, of *Manfred* and *Cain* and the imaginative exercises of Berlioz, Liszt, Mendelssohn, Schumann, Tchaikovsky, Verdi, and the many other composers who made use of the "Byronic Hero" in symphony, opera, and song. Charles Ives clearly had this trend in mind when he denounced Romantic music as committing the "Byronic Fallacy." Nathan's oratorio-style setting of "Saul" prefigures that impact. But the most interesting thing about these *Hebrew Melodies* is really their variety—not, that is, their somber quality, that mourning with which many songs are drenched, but rather the light, ironic touches, the waltz steps, and even the martial and exhortative notes of songs like "Warriors and Chiefs!"

Nathan's settings divide themselves into four categories:

A. Hymns
B. Martial songs
C. German and Italian styles
D. Songs of Jewish "wildness and pathos"

That the individual songs fall comfortably within these groups, although there is occasional ambiguity, gives credence to Nathan's own description of his intentions as a composer: to write songs that were martial, melancholy, reverent, etc. It is important to bear in mind that the triumphs of Brahms's "Wie rafft ich mich auf in der Nacht," or Schubert's great through-composed songs (he wrote one hundred "durchkomponierte Lieder" in the summer and fall of 1815), much less Schumann's "Widmung," or "Mondnacht," were little known or yet to be. Indeed, London was a place where more Italian songs were being published than anything else, rivaling the presses in Italy itself. Thus, the ideal of coequal voice and piano parts was not well defined.

The Italian style tended to have a fully worked-out accompaniment, not necessarily related (except in a general way) to the spirit of the lyric, and a distinctive postlude often making use of materials from the vocal line. While ornamentation was gradually diminishing, it was still expected that vocalists would embroider the melody freely with a trill, appoggiatura, or turn, and pause at the final cadence, often introducing a more extended cadenza. One sees those influences at work in most of Nathan's settings, another proof that "national airs" were but an aspect of the explosion in music publishing in Vienna and London occasioned by the rise of a moneyed middle class. The question we most want answered is, of course, how Nathan's choices capitalized upon or neglected possibilities in the musical material. Israel Abrahams has expressed his disappointment that Nathan ignored possibilities in Sephardic music.[57] But the Sephardic defection, encouraged by the Mendelssohnian movement and a longer London history of secular education and cultural assimilation, would not have strengthened Nathan's confidence in their store of "Ancient" music. The London Ashkenazim, or "Dutch Jews," had kept their Talmud Torah school at the Great Synagogue since 1732 and had resisted the advent of the "Free Schools" (founded in Westminster, 1811, and East End, 1817). Since Nathan was searching for traditional authenticity, it is only natural that he turned to the Ashkenazim rather than the Sephardim. Before chastising the composer for allowing possible sources to slip through his fingers, we ought to assess what he has actually accomplished. It will be apparent from the following analysis that Nathan used his raw material to create themes and variations, that his settings were generally based on clear stylistic goals, and that they now seem consistently apt, especially given the models from which he worked and the expectations of his audience.

A. HYMNS

There are two hymns included in the 1815–16 edition of *Hebrew Melodies*. The numbers in parentheses indicate the song's place in the original order of twenty-four songs:

On Jordan's Banks (6)
From the last Hill (22)

As we have already mentioned, "On Jordan's Banks" uses the tune *Ma'oz tzur*, a Chanukah melody and the source of Luther's hymn. To realize that this is intended to be taken in the same genre as its ancestors is to hear the setting in an entirely different way than it was heard by Nathan's critics, Cohen, Idelsohn, and Abrahams. The lines beginning "The Baal adorers," for example, seem insipid if one expects the music to rise to the content with dramatic forcefulness. But conceived as a hymn, the setting works. Nathan adjusts the time value of the notes to accommodate changes in the syllable count of lines in later stanzas, a practice which he follows in most of his strophic songs, and which he extended in the revision of 1824–29. "From the last Hill that looks on thy once holy Dome" is an elegiac lament more obviously appropriate to the hymnal treatment Nathan gives it. The tune is, however, less recognizably *limited* by the consideration motivating most hymn writers: that there should be nothing out of the ordinary to distract or trip up the amateur vocalist. Both these settings are simple, but "From the last Hill" is a finer piece, particularly because of the way it moves into the minor key and then reemerges onto the short plateau of its own opening melody:

The technique employed here by Nathan is worth noting: the modal shift (rather than modulation) from C minor to the relative major (E flat). This shift is typical of synagogue practice then and now.

B. MARTIAL SONGS

The second category includes five songs, one of which seems to fall on the border line between march and hymn—an ambiguity that need not have worked to disadvantage, but did:

The Harp the Monarch Minstrel Swept (2)
Thy Days are done (11)
Warriors and Chiefs! (13)
The Destruction of Sennacherib (18)
Bright Be the Place of thy Soul (additional songs)

We have already suggested in what lay Nathan's failing in setting "Thy Days are done." The song starts off adequately, though even the first phrases are not forceful enough. Soon, its energy has become diffuse. It intends to embody the meaning, but falls short by allowing itself to be too much stylistically constricted by a hymnal treatment. The other examples of the martial type fare much better, if one has a taste for either the marching variety or the compelling saga—the sort of thing found in "The Destruction of Sennacherib."

This latter song is one of the nicer set-pieces in *Hebrew Melodies*. Deliberately smoothing over the anapestic regularity of the lyric with half notes in the opening measures, Nathan concludes the line "trippingly," then brings in the second line of the lyric ("And his cohorts," etc.) with a galloping triplet accompaniment that runs to the end of the fourth line. This section he concludes with a portentous melody that rides above the busy piano part with a simple half and quarter note line. Then he shifts (as he did in

"From the last Hill") from G minor to—not the relative major, but E flat major. This signals the lyric's shift in mood. Indeed, Nathan's setting of this poem shows a fine sensitivity to the poem's mood and rhythm. Note the way he repeats the line "when autumn hath blown" to darken the song. Underneath, the accompaniment has subsided on the word "blown" from its embroidery in sixteenth notes (begun with the brighter moment of "the leaves in the forest when summer is green" and the shift to the major key) to a chordal pattern. "The Destruction of Sennacherib" is a well-crafted strophic song, perhaps the best of the martial group.

"The Harp the Monarch Minstrel Swept" and "Warriors and Chiefs!" are different from "The Destruction of Sennacherib" in that they adopt a tone of exhortation. The songs proceed deliberately and ostentatiously:

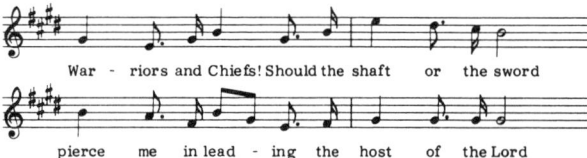

"The Harp the Monarch Minstrel Swept" was written more for solo performance, as it winds its way upward with the lines "It softened men," stopping at plateaus along the way:

It then becomes increasingly complex. The strophe is so long that it can be repeated without becoming hymnal. "Warriors and Chiefs!," though more difficult, lies within reach of the amateur voice, but the singer should resist trumpeting.

"Bright be the Place of thy Soul" is an orphan of the Hebrew Melodies project. It was published as sheet music in June of 1815, and was never (to our knowledge) reprinted, even in the expanded version of 1824–29. It clearly partakes of that exhortative, martial tone we hear in "Warriors and Chiefs" and "The Harp the Monarch Minstrel Swept." Yet its structure more resembles that of "She Walks in Beauty Like the Night," for it repeats the first line of each stanza at the end of the strophe, and the melody includes an interlude. Since Nathan tells us that Byron wrote these stanzas extemporaneously for the music (*FP,* 114), we must assume he rearranged the music for the strophic repetition—perhaps he was impressed with Byron's fondness for "She Walks in Beauty" and sought to emulate his earlier success.

C. THE GERMAN AND ITALIAN STYLES

Our third category is a large one, and consists of three subcategories:

1. Italian Ornamentation
    She Walks in Beauty (1)
    Jephtha's Daughter (7)
    It is the Hour (12)
    Herod's Lament for Mariamne (16)
    Fame, Wisdom, Love, and Power (21)
    They say that Hope is Happiness (additional songs)
    I Speak Not—I Trace Not (additional songs)
2. German Lieder Model
    My Soul is Dark (9)
    Were my Bosom as false (1815–16) (17)
    When Coldness wraps (20)
    Sun of the Sleepless! (24)
    Were my Bosom as false (1824–29) (additional songs)
3. Oratorio
    Thou whose Spell (Saul) (19)
    A Spirit Pass'd (additional songs)

The songs added in 1824–29 and included among the additional songs were all published in the last of four numbers. In fact, of the last ten songs of the 1824–29 edition, *eight* fall into the German/Italian category. Of the songs that were published in the first edition, all but two in this category appeared in the *second* number. Nathan obviously de-emphasized them by their placement, though that does not mean he was less proud of them. Indeed, they were as necessary to the financial success of the venture as the consciously "Hebrew" songs we will discuss in Category D, perhaps more important, if sheer number be the criterion. The large representation of foreign sources in the second number of *Hebrew Melodies* (1816) caused one reviewer to remark that he found them too "Italianated" (*Critical Review* 5th series, III, April 1816, p. 366).

The songs vary considerably in quality and interest. In general they attempt to appropriate what one reviewer called "the noblest and sublimest efforts of modern music to the sacred poetry" (William Roberts, *British Review,* August 1815). "She Walks in Beauty" manages to avoid the trills and chirrups that characterize most of the Italianated melodies listed above. It is simply done, and modulates in a predictable and satisfying way. We have already noted that this piece is exceptional in the volume—and the fact that it makes use of a recognized synagogue tune gives it just that sort of ambiguity that makes any categorization seem arbitrary; but it clearly achieves harmonic and melodic goals that fit what Nathan knew as Italian compositional practice, the kind of thing Corri had taught him.

"Jephtha's Daughter" is a much simpler construction, and its piano accompaniment is more typical of the public-spirited displays that characterize the songs in the martial category. But Nathan has cast the daughter in the dramatic role of operatic heroine. To tighten the rise to a climactic fourth stanza, he omits the second stanza (which might be sung repeating the score for the first stanza) and allows the fifth stanza to recapitulate the opening (a factor that prompted the deletion of the second stanza). The daughter speaks not to her prospective executioners but to the nation of which she, Joan of Arc-like, is as much the leader as the father. The melody, which asseverates, surely must have come from Nathan's research, though no specific source has been located. We have already suggested that it is a form of the *Shir Hashirim,* sung in many Middle Eastern communities even today. But the path by which this music arrived in London in 1815 is unknown. There may be another source, yet undiscovered, but it is extremely unlikely that Nathan came up with this melody out of his own head. It is recognizable neither as a type of the music popular in the period, nor as typically Jewish (to the ears of the gentile population that made up Nathan's audience), nor as an imitation of some other composer. It is, strangely enough, probably the most authentically Jewish song in the collection, a straight transcription of a tune Nathan liked. And the lyric, which we have already defended against attacks by those unaware of the music, plays quite skillfully upon the rhythm and the character of the music.

"It is the Hour," "Herod's Lament," and "Fame, Wisdom" reflect more the popular tastes that built the house of Dibdin. Precisely the sort of parlor music *Hebrew Melodies* generally avoids, these three songs are not musically bad, but they sound divorced from their lyrics. "Herod's Lament," particularly, is pretty enough, yet establishes a tone of playfulness in its early measures that ill accords with the motifs of revenge and anguish expressed in the words. It moves closer to the content on the lines "Oh Mariamne! Where art thou?" But elsewhere it seems to be going through motions independently of the meaning. "It is the Hour," though lightweight, is closer to the lyric's imagined scene. Aside from "She Walks in Beauty," it is the only song in Category C that appeared in the first volume of 1815. The setting is well crafted, and compares favorably with attempts by Braham and others to achieve a similar effect with parallel content, like Braham's "Snowy Rose."

Here, if anywhere in *Hebrew Melodies,* one sees the effect of Braham's influence. Braham's name was deleted in the 1824–29 edition. But in the first edition, despite the fact that he had written no music at all, Braham had his name beside Nathan's on every song. That name guaranteed sales. And Braham gave *Hebrew Melodies* its first public performance. One sees in the Italian-style songs some evidence of Nathan's having catered to Braham's gargantuan appetite for cadenzas. Arguing that Braham "frittered away extraordinary powers of declamation and pathos on trivialities and vulgarities and used his magnificent talents only as a way of acquiring money," one critic tells an anecdote of Braham's departing from his usual manner and singing "in the most perfect artistic style" for a private entertainment as a guest of the Duke of Sussex: "'Why Braham,' said the Duke, 'why don't you always sing like that?' 'If I did,' was the reply, 'I should not have the honor of entertaining your royal highness tonight.'"[58]

But in the general trend of revision, what ornamentation there was in the first edition tended to be reduced in the second, so that Braham's presence was removed along with his name. And even that presence was never substantial, for most of what Braham liked to do was embroidery on whole notes or fermatas. Nathan expressed his feelings about Braham's posturing in *Musurgia Vocalis* through the persona of an anonymous "critic":

I once saw a witty critique on an eminent singer, who, from a mistaken desire to please the million, was often, against his better judgment, extravagantly profuse in his cadences. . . . "The house was crowded, and excessively hot: finding myself overpowered by the heat, I took a walk around Covent Garden to cool myself; when I returned into the theatre, to my utter astonishment, I found Mr. ****** just concluding a cadence on the note on which he was pausing when I quitted the theatre." (*Musurgia Vocalis,* p. 72)

It was with the specific plan of avoiding such *gaucherie* that Nathan conceived the idea of *Hebrew Melodies.* But he did not entirely avoid the trap.

"Fame, Wisdom," "They say that Hope," and "I Speak Not" exhibit the same sort of divorce from the spirit of this project and its lyrics that disturb us in "Herod's Lament." All have that characteristic preoccupation with trilling:

To be fair, the two songs added in 1824–29 ("They say that Hope" and "I Speak Not") have lyrics less clearly related to the ostensible theme. The case of "Fame, Wisdom" grows dim when one considers singing the last two verses to the proffered melody. Here Nathan seems genuinely to have lost an opportunity with the lyric.

The German style, moodier and less ornamented, gave Nathan problems, but seems to have brought out strengths in him as well. His setting of "Sun of the Sleepless!," for example, compares favorably with that of Mendelssohn. Nathan's "Sun of the Sleepless!," playing on the same rhythmic patterns of Mendelssohn's, embroiders the lyric, making the opening phrase a stentorian announcement. Nathan followed what he believed to be the principles of *current* German composition—a soulfulness not muddled by too much ornamentation, but indistinguishable, at times, from the "Italianated" music of the London stage. It is interesting, for example, that when he revised "Sun of the Sleepless!" for the 1824–29 edition, he eliminated a great deal of the baroque exposition of 1815–16. This:

became this:

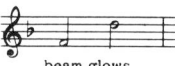

In every case, the songs in this category pass from greater to lesser ornamentation as Nathan reworks them for the second edition, reflecting, perhaps, Nathan's awareness of the changes wrought in German music, but also his awareness that tastes had changed, an awareness Braham resisted. Thus, he consciously sought to reduce the baroque ornamentation and increase touches of what we would now recognize as the evolving form of the Romantic *Lieder*. In this particular case, the changes, small in themselves, combine to create an almost completely different song, and so we have included it in the additional songs for comparison with the original version.

That Nathan was not quite sure how to get the effect he wanted seems clear from the fact that he verges sometimes into folk music. We have already noted how "My Soul is Dark" borrows a bit of the playfulness of "The Wild Gazelle" in its opening bars and how ambiguous is the setting of "Were my Bosom as false." This latter song is the only one Nathan completely rewrote, starting from scratch, when he brought out his second edition in the years 1824–29. Trying to make the piano an equal partner in the first version, Nathan wrote an accompaniment with chromatic cadenzas in 64th notes punctuating the vocalist's lines (see pp. 86 ff.). Apparently distressed by the reception of this ironic use of the love song to underscore the Jew's bitter questioning of his persecutor's posture of superiority, he wrote a second setting that attempts to do the job by more conventional means. The second version is in 3/2 time, and it has the look, but not the sound, of "In the Valley of Waters" (see discussion that follows). The accompaniment is chordal, for the most part, and the melody, too, owes its structure to chordal thinking:

This second version still has stylistic intentions that go unrealized. Nathan was comfortable enough with the Italian mode, but here he encountered real troubles crafting the music.

Not so with the final subcategory of this section, songs based on Handelian oratorio. "A Spirit Pass'd Before Me" is decently made, and "Thou whose Spell" (retitled "Saul" in 1829) is a genuine victory. "A Spirit Pass'd" makes effective use of one of the devices that function so well in "Thou whose Spell"—syncopation:

As in "Were my Bosom" (earlier version), he employs chromatic passages, but this time with greater effect. He makes the accompaniment "creep" with the *flesh* mentioned in the lyric:

The andantino section is a bit of a letdown, however, as it repeats "Heedless and Blind" ten times without the necessary musical development to carry it off.

"Thou whose Spell" does not get into the same troubles, even though it is the longest and the most ambitious undertaking of *Hebrew Melodies*. It is not one but three pieces: A trio, followed by a recitativo and an aria. The trio was expanded in the second edition to a five-voice setting for two sopranos, a tenor and countertenor, and bass. Availing himself of the dramaturgy of the oratorio, Nathan rose to this occasion and gave a richly Handelian setting to Byron's poem. The voices echo and re-echo in the trio, coming together on the one phrase before moving to the next. The recitative is meant to be sung with a good deal of latitude. Short and impressive, it begins with the line "Why is my sleep disquieted" that Byron delighted to repeat. The aria begins in common time and stately fashion, mourning:

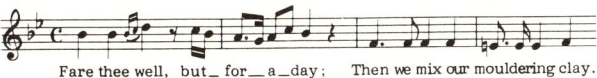

Then it briefly switches to ¾ time and takes off "Presto." It rises rapidly to double *forte*, renders the lines in staccato fashion marked by rests—here is the syncopation also employed in "A Spirit Pass'd"—and straddles the up- and downbeats:

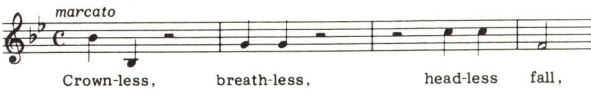

It comes to a breathless conclusion on "son and sire":

The piano then marks its own conclusion with a simple modulation marked double pianissimo. Pyrotechnics like this had a great impact not only on Byron, and this particular song stands up well. The labors Nathan expended upon it are, however, merely easier to detect than those he gave to the most important single category of song in the project, those that attempt to put on "Jewishness."

D. SONGS OF JEWISH "WILDNESS AND PATHOS"

This last category includes eight of the original twenty-four songs published in 1815–16. They break down into two types:

1. Sacred Type
    We sate down (14)
    In the Valley of Waters (additional songs)
2. Gypsy Type
    If that High World (3)
    The Wild Gazelle (4)
    Oh! Weep for Those (5)
    Oh Snatch'd Away (8)
    I saw thee Weep (10)
    Vision of Belshazzar (15)
    Francisca (23)

The first category includes two songs that obviously rely upon the rhythms and vocal lines of the motet writers, like Lassus. The effect is adulterated, but the appeal is clearly to formal lamentation. Both settings are multivoice: "In the Valley of Waters" is a trio and "We sate down" a duet. The music thus owes nothing directly to the "Hebrewness" described below, but it belongs in this category because it attempts to evoke the stereotypical figure of the suffering Jew, like the modern round "By the Waters of Babylon":

In the seven songs of the "Gypsy" type, Nathan played much more directly and obviously to a *musical* stereotype. The settings do not really harp upon the stereotype, nor do they necessarily sustain it through the whole piece, but they are characterized by recognizable musical gestures. They are colored occasionally with tinctures of Oriental harmony Nathan evokes by using the scale of the harmonic minor with its tone and a half step. They also often make use of dance rhythm and strive for an incantational effect. Many of these songs brought reviewers within their sway. The *European Magazine* was impressed (LXVIII, July 1815, p. 37), and so was the *Theatrical Inquisitor*, which described the music of the first number of 1815 as "wild and sweet" (VI, May 1815, pp. 377–78). The reviewer for the *Gentleman's Magazine* was anxious to point out that the music's "interesting wildness of character leaves no doubt of its antiquity" (June 1815). All these writers were responding to Nathan's having successfully evoked a stereotypical figure for them: the Gypsy Jew standing beside Babel's waters, dancing in the desert, appealing to Jehovah for deliverance. It is important to note that a song making use of synagogue material does not automatically fall into this final category. "She Walks in Beauty," for example, though it is in waltz time, though it employs a synagogue tune, is not such a one as "Oh! Weep for Those." First of all, it is in a major key. Eight of the nine songs listed in this final category are composed in the minor. "She Walks in Beauty" does not, most importantly, create a dramatic effect or pose. It is a *mannered* composition, but not self-consciously dramatic, as are the other songs here considered.

Look at the opening bars of "Oh! Weep for Those":

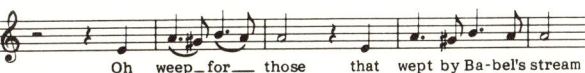

This simple musical phrase is repeated six times with slight ornamentation. At the conclusion of the sequence, Nathan marks the passage with the harmonic minor—a bit of the Middle East on his canvas:

Thereafter, the song shifts in rhythm, as though the opening had been a prelude to this stately dance:

And where shall Is-rael lave her bleed-ing feet

Finishing the dancelike section, Nathan again marks the passage with that characteristic tone-and-a-half step:

Tribes of the wand-'ring foot and wea-ry breast

Then he finishes his composition by treating the lines "Israel but the grave" in grandiose fashion, and he brings back the opening theme not in the voice but in the piano accompaniment:

but the grave.

The piece is neatly executed. It also models an appeal to the audience's image of the "Israelite"—a *musical* appeal—that other songs emulate.

The fact that the song appeals to a stereotype does not mean its techniques are necessarily caricatured or bogus. "Oh! Weep for Those," which is based on a blessing chant, makes use of genuine synagogue melodic patterns—some of which are reminiscent of the Kol Nidre tune. Many of the ornaments in "Vision of Belshazzar" appear to be based upon typical improvisational cadences Nathan might have heard and even used himself as a cantor in London:

Satraps throng'd the hall;— A thou-sand bright lamps shone

"If that High World" employs a melody sung for the Kaddish, a part of the daily ritual of the synagogue in which thanksgiving and praise are offered, together with a prayer for universal peace. The song is filled with cadenza and near-cadenza figures. For example, when the lyric focuses our attention upward toward the light of eternity, the melody complies, using a figure like that of "Vision of Belshazzar," but with its interval inverted:

soar__ from__ earth__ and__ find__ all__ fears__

"I saw thee Weep" and "Oh Snatch'd Away," both in 6/8 time, adopt, not the visionary, but the mourning pose most characteristic of these songs, even including "The Wild Gazelle," which starts off and ends on a note of celebration, but in between works the same ground of anguish. "I saw thee Weep" has a particular effect that we have noted before:

Nathan *shifts* rather than modulates, and the melodic line suggests a scale not exactly the harmonic minor, but not precisely the melodic minor or major either:

dew,__ A Vio-let drop-ping dew, I saw thee smile

The song has been dancelike from the very beginning, but this unusual passage transforms the controlled beginning into freer interpretation. After this, the harmony will make its way back to the G minor opening.

"Oh Snatch'd Away," too, makes use of the dance image. Less folk-oriented than "I saw thee Weep," it dramatizes the text by varying and ornamenting its melody. It begins with an up-tempo sweep to the octave ("If that High World" makes use of a similar gambit in a different rhythm):

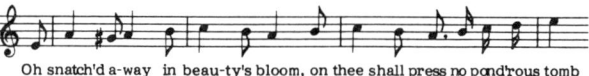
Oh snatch'd a-way in beau-ty's bloom, on thee shall press no pond'rous tomb

It then turns to twining variations on the stanza's final phrase:

and the wild cy-press wave_____ in

Presumably, the singer should sway with the wild cypress. By ironing out the sixteenth note in the repetition, Nathan uses a technique that serves him in other songs in this category: He moves from more to less busy melodic lines. In this particular song he does it again on a grander scale when he shifts in response to the lyric from A minor to G major—again, the technique of shifting rather than modulating comes into play. Later, he changes the time signature from 6/8 to common time and *modulates* back to A minor. These rhythmic and harmonic changes introduce the effect of coming out onto calm sea from rough water. Busyness always threatens to creep back in, but before it can get going, Nathan moves on. Before the final section of "Oh Snatch'd Away," the composer once again touches the familiar scale:

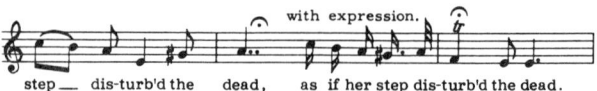
step__ dis-turb'd the dead, as if her step dis-turb'd the dead.

And, as in "Oh! Weep for Those," he returns to the opening theme in a solo piano passage.

Through such staple effects as shifts in mode, dance rhythms, tone-and-a-half steps, and cantillatory ornaments, Nathan creates a stereotypically Jewish effect. One hears the same techniques at work in "The Wild Gazelle" and "Francisca." "Francisca" is in 6/8 time. It begins in F minor, and its opening suggests a chant. Then it moves away and begins to ornament rather heavily. In its final measures it even capitalizes on the syncopation and

Introduction / 36

"breathlessness" that characterize the aria of "Thou whose Spell." Yet its opening measures mark it as fundamentally different in intention from the Italian and German songs, from the oratorio-style settings. "The Wild Gazelle," too, has some fairly heavy baroque touches, but its F minor interlude and the lilt of its opening phrases mark it similarly as a dramatic piece on the Gypsy model.

The quality of *Hebrew Melodies* must be judged on the merits of performance. But judgment is conditioned by expectations, and, as we have shown, Nathan's purpose was not the narrow one so many have assumed. He was not content to endear the players of the parlor piano nor to delight a concert audience for a season. He did certainly misrepresent the age of the music's sources, but he had a true sense for the power of Jewish music. Like Byron, too, Nathan expected to be treated as an upstart. He sought scholarly validation for the project not merely to enrich his purse, but to put Jewish music on an equal footing with Scottish, Welsh, and Irish, to show it was as susceptible of varied treatments, as "wild" and strange, and as sweet and familiar. He had never defined narrowly his musical roots. In *Musurgia Vocalis* he openly admired German and Italian "perfection," and he placed Handel's hymns on a pedestal; he also referred to Oriental and Jewish sources evenhandedly with Christian.

Byron's collaboration with Nathan called for a peculiar partnership; certainly there were mixed motives on both sides, and Nathan finally faced a difficult choice among ethnic integrity, good music, and financial success. He sought all, but needed (as one might expect) money first, letting quality come second and Jewishness third. Despite this, his work is often excellent and does retain a significant musicological interest. Byron, for his part, liked playing friend to Nathan, and it is tempting to praise his open-mindedness, comparing him with crude Kinnaird and jealous Moore. Byron's letters, however, repeat most of the racist invectives against Jewish moneylenders. His involvement in the Zionist themes of *Hebrew Melodies* did not free him of prejudice. Nor was he able to avoid his own hard choices concerning money, success, and artistic integrity. He was motivated strongly enough by *noblesse oblige* to stoop to involvement with Nathan—becoming more involved than he intended, and more than has yet been realized, since criticism has continued to ignore this chapter in history at the cost of an enriched appreciation of the *Hebrew Melodies*.

Notes to Introduction

1. This facsimile edition of *A Selection of Hebrew Melodies* (London: C. Richards, 1815–1816), is a photographic reproduction of the copy in the private collection of Mr. and Mrs. Jack G. Wasserman, New York, New York.

2. Thomas L. Ashton, *Byron's Hebrew Melodies* (Austin: University of Texas Press, 1972), pp. 3–61.

3. Jerome J. McGann, ed., *Lord Byron: The Complete Poetical Works,* III (Oxford: Clarendon Press, 1983), 249–272 (text) and 465–472 (commentary).

4. Geoffrey Bush and Nicholas Temperley, eds., *English Songs: 1800–1860,* in *Musica Britannica: A National Collection of Songs,* XLIII (London: Stainer and Bell, 1979), p. xviii. Bush and Temperley imply that Braham was not a "musician's musician," and that "his" works were therefore left out of their volume. Yet they note that Byron's verses were set by many other composers, and that a general reaching out for the exotic—especially the Oriental—followed the appearance of the *Hebrew Melodies*.

5. Myer Lyon, Braham's uncle, also performed in opera, but had a limited stage career even after his successful debut as Arbaces in *Artaxerxes* at Covent Garden (25 April 1775). Braham and his uncle were choristers at the same time at the Great Synagogue in London, and many claimed Lyon had the "sweeter" voice; John M. Levien, *The Singing of John Braham* (London: Novello, 1945), pp. 1–8.

6. Todd M. Endelman, *The Jews of Georgian England, 1714–1830: Tradition and Change in a Liberal Society* (Philadelphia: Jewish Publication Society, 1979), p. 271.

7. Ibid., p. 112.

8. Geoffrey Alderman, *The Jewish Community in British Politics* (Oxford: Clarendon Press, 1983), pp. 10–12.

9. Endelman, *Jews of Georgian England,* pp. 259–260.

10. Isaac Nathan and Elizabeth Rosetta Worthington were married twice: first an Anglican marriage (16 July 1812), then a Jewish marriage in a London synagogue three months later, where Elizabeth Rosetta was registered on the *ketubah* as a convert to the Jewish faith. Both Olga Somech Phillips, *Isaac Nathan: Friend of Byron* (London: Minerva, 1940), and Catherine Mackerras, *The Hebrew Melodist, A Life of Isaac Nathan* (Sydney: Currawong, 1963), call the marriage an "elopement." Marriage banns, however, were duly announced, and the marriage was recorded in the parish register of St. Mary Abbot's, Kensington, Middlesex, entry no. 461: "Isaac Nathan of this parish BATCHELOR and Rosetta Elizabeth Worthington [*sic*] of this parish SPINSTER were married in this CHURCH by BANNS this 16th Day of July in the year One Thousand Eighthundred and Twelve by me Henry Taylor." Elizabeth Rosetta Nathan died in childbirth at Nelson Square, London (19 January 1824) and was buried at the Jewish Cemetery at St. Alban's. The five surviving children were baptized in the Church of England; Lady Caroline Lamb was their godmother.

11. Charles Lamb, "Imperfect Sympathies," *Essays of Elia,* in *Works,* 12 vols., ed. Alfred Ainger (Boston: Merrymount Press, 1888), II, 115–116.

12. William Hazlitt, *Complete Works,* ed. P. P. Howe (London: Dent, 1930–34), XVIII, 289. Drama review, *London Magazine* (February 1820).

13. Quoted in Phillips, *Isaac Nathan: Friend of Byron,* p. 85.

14. Isaac Nathan, *Fugitive Pieces and Reminiscences of Lord Byron,* (London: Whittaker, Treacher, and Co., 1829), pp. 147–196, recounts his concert performances for Lady Caroline Lamb. At the very time he commenced his collaboration with Lord Byron in 1814, he was also composing for Lady Caroline Lamb. At least two of her songs Nathan had published as sheet music: "My

Heart's Fit to Break" and "The Kiss that's on thy Lip impressed." His patriotic pieces, "Wellington's Return" and "The Hero of Aix," were performed at Vauxhall Gardens.

15. Corri's book, *The Singer's Preceptor: Or, Corri's Treatise on Vocal Music* (London: Chappell and Co., 1810), has been published in a facsimile edition with Nathan's own *Musurgia Vocalis* (London: Whittaker, 1823) as a volume titled *The Porpora Tradition,* ed. Edward Foreman (Pro Musica Press, 1968), Vol. III of *Masterworks on Singing.*

16. In addition to the assistance of Charles Venour Nathan in consulting unpublished family records, we have drawn from several published accounts of Nathan's career: Olga Somech Phillips, Catherine Mackerras, and Thomas L. Ashton, cited above; Charles H. Bertie, *Isaac Nathan: Australia's First Composer* (Sydney: Angus & Robertson, Ltd., 1922); Edward Rimbault Dibdin, "Isaac Nathan," *Music and Letters* XXII (1941), pp. 75-80.

17. J. Cuthbert Hadden, *George Thomson* (London: J. C. Nimmo, 1898), p. 191.

18. Leon Plantinga, *Romantic Music: A History of Musical Styles in Nineteenth-Century Europe* (New York: W. W. Norton, 1984), p. 398; see also: Rey M. Longyear, *Nineteenth-Century Romanticism in Music* (Englewood Cliffs, N.J.: Prentice Hall, 2nd ed. 1973), p. 242.

19. Letters quoted in Phillips, *Isaac Nathan: Friend of Byron,* pp. 38-40.

20. Kinnaird's letters, in the Murray collection, are quoted in Ashton, *Byron's Hebrew Melodies,* p. 21.

21. Leigh Hunt, *Autobiography,* ed. Roger Ingpen, 2 vols. (London: Constable, 1903), I, 140.

22. Isaac Nathan, *Fugitive Pieces and Reminiscences of Lord Byron,* p. 51. Further references to this edition *(FP)* will appear parenthetically in the text. *Fugitive Pieces* reprints in its first 81 pages the notes and commentaries included in the later revised edition of *Hebrew Melodies* published by Nathan in four separate numbers: I and II (1824, 1827); III (1828) and IV (1829).

23. To Annabella Milbanke (20 October 1814), *Byron's Letters and Journals,* ed. Leslie A. Marchand (Cambridge, Mass.: Harvard University Press, 1973-1982), IV, 220. Subsequent references from *BL&J* will be given parenthetically in the text. See also: Ethel Colburn Mayne, *The Life and Letters of Anne Isabella Lady Noel Byron* (London: Constable, 1929), p. 469.

24. Leigh Hunt, *Lord Byron and Some of His Contemporaries* (London: Henry Colburn, 1828), I, 187-188.

25. Samuel Smiles, *A Publisher and His Friends, Memoir and Correspondence of the late John Murray* (London: John Murray, 1891), I, 351.

26. H. J. C. Grierson, et al., eds., *The Letters of Sir Walter Scott* (London: Constable, 1932-37), IV. Nathan's letter to Scott (22 November 1815), in the National Library of Scotland, is quoted in Joseph Slater, "Byron's Hebrew Melodies," *Studies in Philology,* XLIX (1952), 88. Slater gives an excellent brief account of the collaboration between Byron and Nathan and the English reception of *Hebrew Melodies.*

27. Hunt, *Lord Byron,* I, 187-188, and Nathan, *Fugitive Pieces,* p. 87.

28. *Notes from the Letters of Thomas Moore to His Music Publisher, James Power,* ed. Thomas Crofton Croker (New York: J. S. Redfield, 1853), pp. 42-43, 46.

29. In his 1815 catalogue of songs to the poetry of Byron, Nathan advertised the *Hebrew Melodies* along with eleven additional settings: *"Night Wanes" (Lara),* *"This Rose, to calm my Brother's cares" (Bride of Abydos),* *"Yes, love indeed is light from heaven" (The Giaour),* *"Think not thou art what thou appearest" (Bride of Abydos),* *"The Sun's last rays are on the hill" (The Giaour),* *"Ah! were I sever'd from thy side,"* *"The kiss, dear maid, thy lip has left,"* *"Thou art not false, but thou art fickle,"* *"My Life, I love you,"* *"Fair Haidee,"* and *"Bound where thou wilt, my barb."* In the 1829 catalogue bound with *Fugitive Pieces,* Nathan lists six more Byronic songs: "Tambourgi! Tambourgi!" *(Childe Harold,* II), *"Ada" (Childe Harold,* III), "The castled crag of Drachenfels" *(Childe Harold,* III), "As o'er the cold sepulchral stone" ("Lines Written in an Album, at Malta"), *"When we two parted" (Poems,* 1816), and "Well! Thou art happy" *(Hours of Idleness).* From *Hours of Idleness,* Nathan set three more: "This Votive Pledge" ("Stanzas to a Lady with the Poems of Comoëns"), "When friendship or love" ("The Tear"), and "When I rov'd a young highlander." Fourteen of these additional settings (those marked with an asterisk, plus "Bright be the Place of thy Soul") are in the rebound compiler's copy of *A Selection of Hebrew Melodies* (London: C. Richards, 1815-1816), Beinecke Library, Yale University (In. B996/+G815 copy 1); apparently compiled by one of Nathan's pupils, the volume, stamped "Miss Percy 1824," also includes twenty songs Nathan composed to lyrics by Lady Caroline Lamb, Mrs. Wilmot, Robert Harding Evans, and the Rev. J. Davies, among others, and one rondo composed by "Miss M. A. C., pupil to Mr. I. Nathan."

30. William Roberts, *British Review,* VI (August 1815), 200-208. The reviews of *Hebrew Melodies* have been reproduced in *The Romantics Reviewed,* ed. Donald H. Reiman (New York: Garland, 1972), Part B, I-V. Subsequent references to the reviews will be noted parenthetically by periodical and date; consult the bibliography for complete reference.

31. Francis Cohen, "Isaac Nathan," *Jewish Encyclopedia* (New York: Funk and Wagnalls, 1925), vol. IX, p. 179. Abraham Zevi Idelsohn, *Jewish Music in its Historical Development* (New York: Henry Holt and Company, 1929), p. 338. Israel Abrahams, *Bypaths in Hebraic Bookland* (Jewish Publication Society of America, 1920), p. 207.

32. Eric Werner, *A Voice Still Heard: The Sacred Songs of the Ashkenazic Jews* (University Park: Pennsylvania State University Press, 1976), pp. 221, 321.

33. Slater, "Byron's Hebrew Melodies," p. 86.

34. For this information the editors thank Cantor William Sharlin of the Leo Baeck Temple in Westwood, California.

35. Isaac Levy, *Antologia de Liturgia Judeo-Española* (Jerusalem: Haim Ha-Cohen, n.d.), 2 vols., contains several versions of this particular melody.

36. William Roberts documents the argument "that the old Hebrew music was entirely lost" from the account presented in Robert Lowth, *Praelectiones de Sacra Poesi Hebraerorum* (1753; "notas et epimetra adjeci J. D. Michaelis," 1775), XXV. In *Gentleman's Magazine* (June 1815), the argument is cited from Charles Burney, *A General History of Music* (London: privately printed for the author, 1776-1789), I, 224-258; and from Christian Kalkbrenner, *Histoire de la musique* (Paris: Chez A. König, 1804), I, 34. Also citing from Lowth and Burney, Robert Harding Evans built his counter-argument, defending tradition and authenticity, *An Essay on the Music of the Hebrews,* (London: John Booth, 1816), pp. 42-46.

37. Nathan, *Musurgia Vocalis,* p. 190.

38. Heinrich Heine, *Sämtliche Schriften,* ed. Klaus Briegleb (Munich: Carl Hanser Verlag, 1976), I, 801. "Es war der einzige Mensch, mit dem ich mich verwandt fühlte, und wir mögen uns wohl in manchen Dingen geglichen haben. . . . Ich bin . . . mit Byron immer behaglich umgegangen wie mit einem völlig gleichen Spießkameraden."

39. Heine, I, 801. "Ich war jung, mein Freund, fünfundzwanzig Jahre, als meine Brust wiederhallte von der wilden Melancholie Byrons" (*Gespräche,* 1852). See also *Hebräische Melodien,* VI, 124–172 and notes VI$_2$, 58–63.

40. Ashton, *Byron's Hebrew Melodies,* pp. 21-22, summarizes the evidence for dating these poems.

41. *Letters of Moore,* p. 46.

42. Henry Crabb Robinson, *On Books and Their Writers,* ed. Edith J. Morley (London: J. M. Dent and Sons, 1938), I, 372.

43. William Jerdan, *Autobiography* (London: Arthur Hall, Virtue, & Co., 1852–53) I, ch. v.

44. Hobhouse, Diary, 1814–1829; British Museum, Add. MS. 47232, f. 39^v. Quoted in Ashton, *Byron's Hebrew Melodies,* p. 24.

45. Ashton, *Byron's Hebrew Melodies,* pp. 90, 142.

46. Ian Jack, *English Literature, 1815–1832* (Oxford: Clarendon Press, 1963), p. 59.

47. Stith Thompson, *Motif-Index of Folk-Literature* (rev. ed, Bloomington: Indiana University Press, 1955–58) 6 vols.; Johannes Bolte and Georg Polivka, *Anmerkung zu den Kinder- und Hausmärchen der Brüder Grimm* (rev. ed. Hildesheim: Olms, 1963), II, 329, "Verschreibung des Kindes an den Teufel in Unwissenheit."

48. Bruno Bettelheim, *The Uses of Enchantment* (New York: Knopf, 1976), pp. 145–46.

49. McGann, *Lord Byron: The Complete Poetical Works,* III, 471.

50. Byron's pencil note on transcription of (1) "In the Valley of Waters" and (2) "By the Rivers of Babylon" in MS. C: "Dear Kinnaird—Take only one of these marked 1 & 2—as both are but different versions of the *same thought*—leave the choice to any competent person you like." Ashton, *Byron's Hebrew Melodies,* p. 164.

51. Slater, pp. 90–91; Ashton, pp. 72–74. See also: Richard Hurd, *An Introduction to the Study of the Prophecies* (London: J. Nichols for T. Cadell, 1788), pp. 172–187; Joseph Priestley, *Institutes of Natural and Revealed Religion* (Birmingham: Pearson and Rollason for J. Johnson, 1782), II, 420; Moses Margoliouth, *History of the Jews in Great Britain,* 3 vol. (London: R. Bentley, 1851); N. Sokolow, *History of Zionism,* 2 vol. (London: Longmans, Green, 1919).

52. *The Universal Songster* (London: Jones, n.d. [ca. 1830]), II, 9.

53. *The Genuine Works of Flavius Josephus, the Jewish Historian,* trans. William Whiston (London: W. Bowyer, 1737).

54. To Thomas Moore, 28 October 1815; see also Diary, 1821, *BL&J,* III, 232; V, 190.

55. For Byron's further speculations on the immortality of mind/soul, see: Paper Book (Ravenna, 1821) in *BL&J,* V, 456–457. See also: Peter Thorslev, "The Romantic Mind Is Its Own Place," *Comparative Literature,* XV, no. 3 (Summer 1963), 250–268, for discussion of Manfred's appropriation of Satan's thesis: "The mind is its own place, and in itself / Can make a Heav'n of Hell, a Hell of Heav'n" (*Paradise Lost,* I, 251–259; *Manfred,* I, i, 252; III, i, 73; III, iv, 129–132).

56. Leslie A. Marchand, *Byron: A Biography* (New York: Knopf, 1957), I, 107–109.

57. Abrahams, *Bypaths in Hebraic Bookland,* pp. 208–209.

58. William Barclay Squire, "John Braham," *Dictionary of National Biography* (London: Oxford University Press, 1975).

About Performance

Most of these songs are, typically of the period, written for tenor (a medium to high range) voice. One may transpose them, but the character of the song will not go unaffected if the tranposition is more than a tone or two. Also typically of the period, the songs contain very few dynamic marks; Nathan had been trained in the opera tradition of allowing singers almost complete latitude. The vocalist must beware of mistaking a diminuendo (the "hairpin" mark) for an accent, or vice versa.

Slurs are found infrequently, and they are not generally used to indicate phrases. Unless otherwise marked, the vocal line is generally presumed to be legato. Virtually no pedaling marks are found for the pianist, but some dynamic marks in the piano part may help the vocalist.

Nathan has marked more ornaments in his text than are generally found in the music of the period, but the markings are still conservative. The vocalist should actively seek places to embellish with trill, turn, or appoggiatura. Some "ad lib" markings will be found, and these, usually preceding a fermata, indicate the expectation of a brief cadenza. At the final cadence, a pause and slowing would be expected, and a cadenza often invited.

About the Texts

This facsimile edition has been photographed with high-contrast film to filter out paper discoloration ("age spots") in the original editions. The present format has reduced the size of the original editions: the 1815–1816 edition is crown folio trimmed to 34.7 x 24.3 cm.; the 1824–1829 edition is trimmed to 34.5 x 26 cm.

For the 1815–1816 edition, the photographic reproduction is from the copy in the private collection of Mr. and Mrs. Jack G. Wasserman, New York, New York: *A Selection of Hebrew Melodies, Ancient and Modern, with appropriate Symphonies & accompaniments, By I: Braham & I: Nathan, the Poetry written expressly for the work By the Honble Lord Byron* (London: C. Richards, 1815) [an 1816 reissue bound together with] No. II (London: C. Richards, 1816).

For the songs of the 1824–1829 edition (in Additional Songs), the photographic reproduction is from the copy in the Mitchell Library, New South Wales: *A Selection of Hebrew Melodies, Ancient and Modern, Newly arranged Harmonized corrected and Revised*, Nos. I and II (London: J. Fentum, 1824; reprinted 1827); No. III (London: Mary Ann Fentum, 1828); No. IV (London: H. Faulkner 1829).

Nathan's first edition of twelve *Hebrew Melodies* appeared in April 1815, and Murray's edition of twenty-four *Hebrew Melodies* (plus "On the Death of Sir Peter Parker") appeared in May 1815. In April 1816, Nathan reissued the first number of twelve songs bound together with the second number, an additional twelve songs. The four numbers of the 1824–1829 edition includes twenty-eight songs (six in No. I; six in No. II; eight in No. III; eight in No. IV—the four added songs are in this final number). "Bright be the Place of thy Soul," which Nathan includes in his *Fugitive Pieces* (London: Whittaker, Treacher, and Co., 1829), but in neither the 1815–1816 nor the 1824–1829 editions, is reprinted here from the sheet music (London: J. Green, 1815).

This facsimile includes Nathan's settings to twenty-nine *Hebrew Melodies,* with alternate settings to "Sun of the Sleepless!" and "Were My Bosom As False." Only one of the thirty poems identified as belonging to Byron's composition for the *Hebrew Melodies* is excluded: Nathan did not receive a copy of "To Belshazzar," which Byron wrote as an alternative version of "The Vision of Belshazzar."

Both the 1815–1816 and the 1824–1829 editions include the letterpress text of the lyrics printed on lighter stock and interleaved with the engraved accompaniments. Because of the musical phrasing, repetitions, and the strophic structure of Nathan's settings, the interlinear text to the engraved music differs from the letterpress text. While the twelve lyrics of Nathan's first number (April 1815) were used as copy for John Murray's edition (May 1815), the process was reversed when Nathan turned to Murray in preparing the second number (April 1816). Nathan's letterpress text for the first number was newly set for reissue with the second number. Since both editions drew directly from Byron's manuscripts, or from Lady Byron's fair copies, and both benefitted from Byron's corrections, it must be acknowledged that the two editions share authority. The most significant textual difference is that Nathan includes "Francisca" but does not add "A Spirit Pass'd before me" until 1829. Murray includes "A Spirit Pass'd before me" but excludes "Francisca."

Textual changes that are a part of the musical treatment are discussed above in the Introduction and Notes to the songs. For a complete account of the textual variants, the scholar should consult Thomas L. Ashton's variorum edition, *Byron's Hebrew Melodies* (Austin: University of Texas Press, 1972). The standard edition of the poems is Jerome J. McGann, ed., *Lord Byron: The Complete Poetical Works,* III (Oxford: Clarendon Press, 1983), 249–272 (text) and 465–472 (commentary).

A Selection of Hebrew Melodies, Ancient and Modern, by Isaac Nathan and Lord Byron

A Selection of Hebrew Melodies

Ancient and Modern

with appropriate Symphonies & accompaniments

by

I: Braham & I: Nathan

the Poetry written expressly for the work

by the Right Hon.ble

Lord Byron

ent.d at Sta.rs hall  1.st Number

Published & Sold by I: Nathan N.o 7 Poland Street Oxford Str.t

and to be had at the principal Music and Booksellers

Price one Guinea

Drawn by Edward Blore.   *Engraved by W. Lowry.*

John Braham

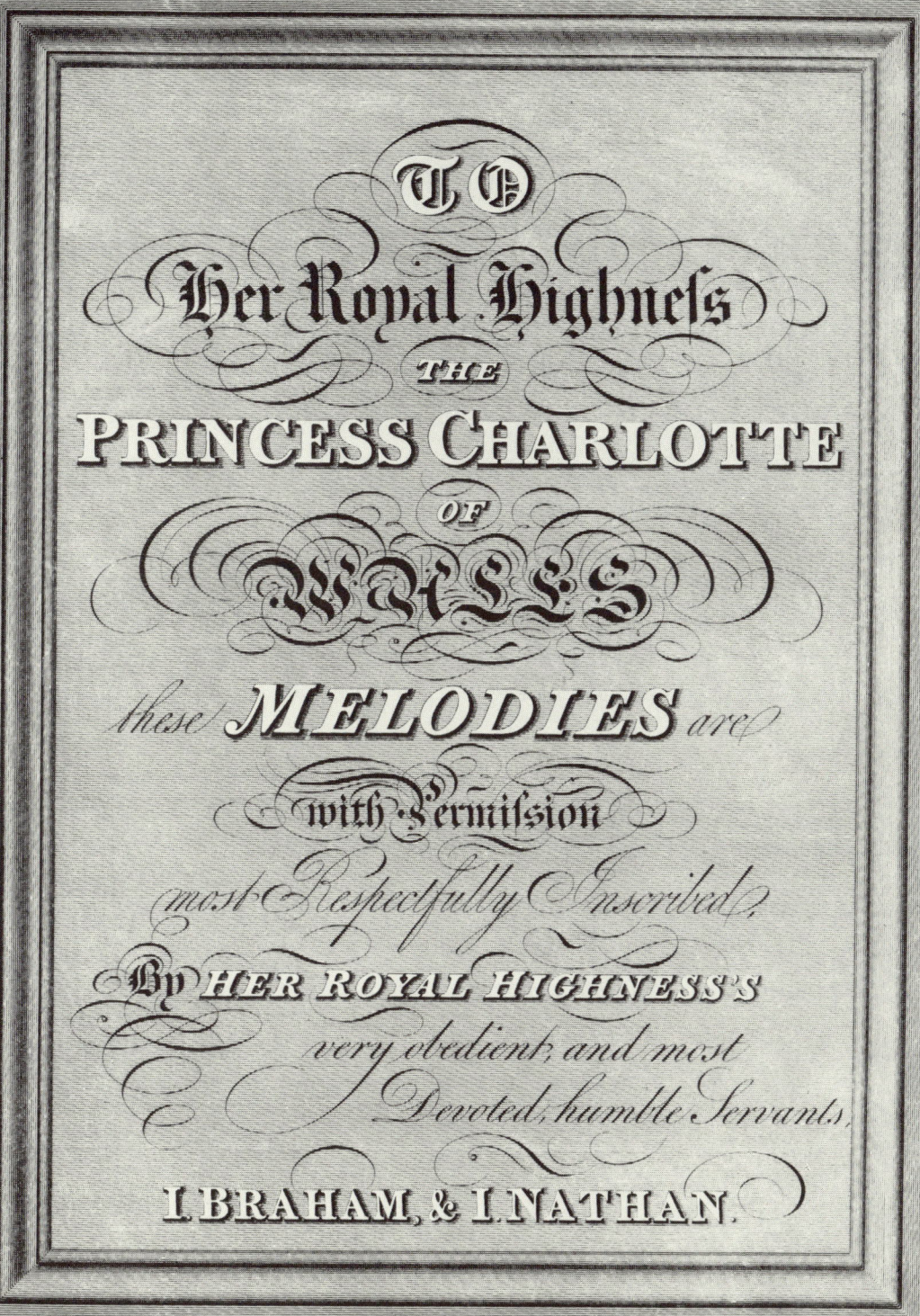

PREFACE.

THE Title under which this Work appears before the PUBLIC, requires that a few words should be said in explanation of what are the pretensions of the Music. " The HEBREW MELODIES" are a Selection from the favourite Airs which are still sung in the religious Ceremonies of the Jews. Some of these have, in common with all their Sacred Airs, been preserved by memory and tradition alone, without the assistance of written characters. Their age and originality, therefore, must be left to conjecture. But the latitude given to the taste and genius of their performers has been the means of engrafting on the original Melodies a certain wildness and pathos, which have at length become the chief characteristic of the Sacred Songs of the Jews.

Of this feature it has been endeavoured to preserve as much as was consistent with the rythm of written Music, and the adaptation of the Words.

Of the Poetry it is necessary to speak, in order thus publicly to acknowledge the kindness with which LORD BYRON has condescended to furnish the most valuable part of the Work. It has been our endeavour to select such Melodies as would best suit the style and sentiment of the Poetry.

I. BRAHAM.
I. NATHAN.

LONDON, *April*, 1815.

INDEX

TO

THE FIRST NUMBER.

	PAGE.
She walks in Beauty	1
The Harp the Monarch Minstrel swept	5
If that high World	14
The wild Gazelle	19
Oh weep for those	25
On Jordan's Banks	29
Jephtha's Daughter	36
Oh snatch'd away in Beauty's Bloom	41
My Soul is dark	44
I saw thee weep	49
Thy Days are done	52
It is the Hour	63

HARMONISED AIRS,

FOR

FOUR VOICES.

	PAGE.
The Harp the Monarch Minstrel swept	8
On Jordan's Banks	31
Thy Days are done	56

N. B. The Second Number will consist of Songs, Duets, and Glees for Three Voices.

SHE WALKS IN BEAUTY.*

I.

SHE walks in beauty—like the night
   Of cloudless climes and starry skies,
And all that's best of dark and bright
   Meet in her aspect and her eyes:
Thus mellow'd to that tender light
   Which heaven to gaudy day denies.
      She walks in beauty—like the night
      Of cloudless climes and starry skies.

II.

One shade the more, one ray the less
   Had half impaired the nameless grace
Which waves in every raven tress,
   Or softly lightens o'er her face—
Where thoughts serenely sweet express
   How pure—how dear their dwelling place.
      She walks in beauty—like the night
      Of cloudless climes and starry skies.

III.

And on that cheek, and o'er that brow
   So soft—so calm—yet eloquent
The smiles that win—the tints that glow
   But tell of days in goodness spent.
A mind at peace with all below—
   A heart whose love is innocent.
      She walks in beauty—like the night
      Of cloudless climes and starry skies.

---

* It may be proper to observe, that this Melody does not differ essentially from the preceding, but as both are sung in different Synagogues, and it is difficult to decide upon their respective claims to originality, we have taken the liberty of publishing them separately.

B. & N.

THE HARP THE MONARCH MINSTREL SWEPT.

I.

THE harp the Monarch Minstrel swept,
    The King of men—the lov'd of Heav'n—
Which Music hallowed while she wept
    O'er tones her heart of hearts had giv'n—
      Redoubled be her tears---its chords are riv'n!
It soften'd men of iron mould,
    It gave them virtues not their own;
No ear so dull---no soul so cold
    That felt not---fired not to the tone,
      Till David's lyre grew mightier than his throne.

II.

It told the triumphs of our King---
    It wafted glory to our God—
It made our gladdened vallies ring—
    The cedars bow---the mountains nod---
Its sound aspired to Heaven and there abode.
Since then---though heard on earth no more---
    Devotion and her daughter Love
Still bid the bursting spirit soar
    To sounds that seem as from above
In dreams that day's broad light can not remove.

Hebrew Melodies / 58

Hebrew Melodies / 60

Hebrew Melodies / 62

IF THAT HIGH WORLD.

I.

IF that high world—which lies beyond
    Our own, surviving love endears,
If there the cherished heart be fond,
    The eye the same—except in tears—
How welcome those untrodden spheres!
    How sweet this very hour to die!
To soar from earth and find all fears
    Lost in thy light—eternity.

II.

It must be so—'tis not for self
    That we so tremble on the brink,
And striving to o'erleap the gulph
    Yet cling to Being's breaking link:
Oh! in that future let us think
    To hold each heart the heart that shares,
With them the immortal waters drink
    And soul in soul grow deathless theirs!

THE WILD GAZELLE.

I.

THE wild Gazelle on Judah's hills
    Exulting yet may bound,
And drink from all the living rills
    That gush on holy ground—
Its airy step and glorious eye
May glance in tameless transport by—

II.

A step as fleet—an eye more bright
    Hath Judah witness'd there—
And o'er her scenes of lost delight
    Inhabitants more fair—
The cedars wave on Lebanon,
But Judah's statelier maids are gone.

III.

More blest each palm that shades those plains
    Than Israel's scattered race;
For taking root it there remains
    In solitary grace.
It cannot quit its place of birth,
It will not live in other earth.

IV.

But we must wander witheringly
    In other lands to die—
And where our fathers' ashes be
    Our own may never lie.
Our temple hath not left a stone
And mockery sits on Salem's throne.

OH WEEP FOR THOSE.

I.

OH weep for those that wept by Babel's stream,

Whose shrines are desolate, whose land a dream,

Weep for the harp of Judah's broken shell—

Mourn—where their God hath dwelt—the Godless dwell!

II.

And where shall Israel lave her bleeding feet?

And when shall Zion's songs again seem sweet?

And Judah's melody once more rejoice

The hearts that leap'd before its heavenly voice?

III.

Tribes of the wandering foot and weary breast!

How shall ye flee away and be at rest?

The wild-dove hath her nest—the fox his cave—

Mankind their Country—Israel but the grave.

ON JORDAN'S BANKS.

I.

ON Jordan's banks the Arabs' camels stray,

On Sion's hill the false-one's votaries pray,

The Baal-adorer bows on Sinai's steep—

Yet there—even there—Oh God! thy thunders sleep.

II.

There—where thy finger scorch'd the tablet stone,

There—where thy Shadow to thy people shone!

Thy Glory shrouded in its garb of fire:—

Thyself—none living see and not expire!—

III.

Oh! in the lightning—let thy glance appear!

Sweep from his shiver'd hand the oppressor's spear:

How long by tyrants shall thy land be trod!

How long thy temple worshipless! Oh God?

Hebrew Melodies / 80

"On Jordan's banks."

Nathan.

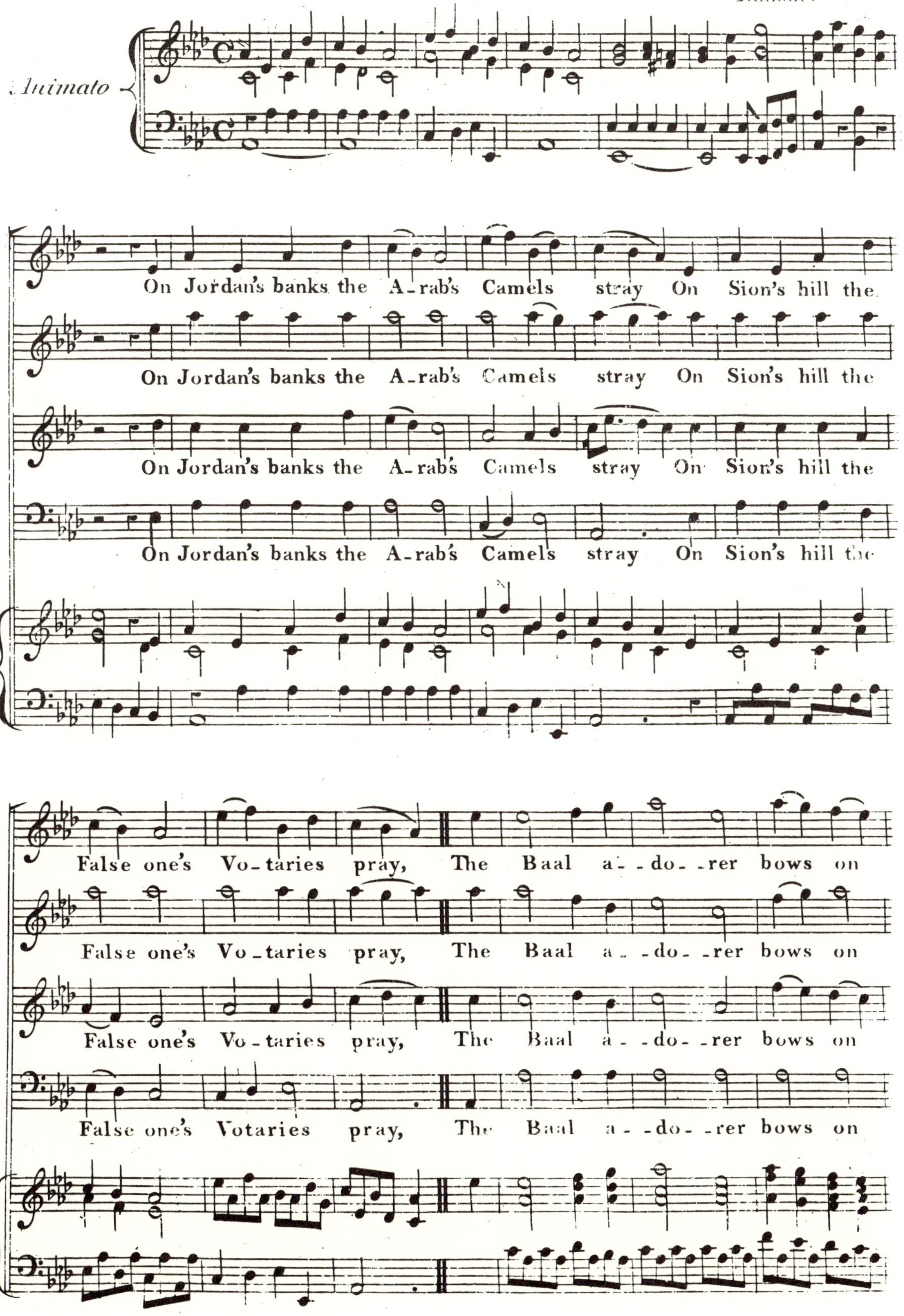
Animato
On Jordan's banks the A_rab's Camels stray On Sion's hill the
On Jordan's banks the A_rab's Camels stray On Sion's hill the
On Jordan's banks the A_rab's Camels stray On Sion's hill the
On Jordan's banks the A_rab's Camels stray On Sion's hill the
False one's Vo_taries pray, The Baal a_-do_-rer bows on
False one's Vo_taries pray, The Baal a_-do_-rer bows on
False one's Vo_taries pray, The Baal a_-do_-rer bows on
False one's Votaries pray, The Baal a_-do_-rer bows on

Hebrew Melodies / 85

Hebrew Melodies / 87

JEPHTHA'S DAUGHTER.

I.

SINCE our Country—our God—Oh my Sire—
Demand that thy daughter expire;
Since thy triumph was bought by thy vow—
Strike the bosom that's bared for thee now!

II.

And the voice of my mourning is o'er—
And the mountains behold me no more:
If the hand that I love, lay me low,
There cannot be pain in the blow!

III.

And of this—Oh! my Father—be sure
That the blood of thy child is as pure—
As the blessing I beg 'ere it flow—
And the last thought that soothes me below.

IV.

Though the virgins of Salem lament,
Be the Judge and the Hero unbent!
I have won the great battle for thee,
And my Father and Country are free!

V.

When this blood of thy giving hath gush'd—
When the voice that thou lovest is hush'd—
Let my Memory still be thy pride,
And forget not, I smiled as I died.

OH! SNATCH'D AWAY IN BEAUTY'S BLOOM.

I.

OH! snatch'd away in beauty's bloom!
On thee shall press no ponderous tomb,
   But on thy turf shall roses rear
   Their leaves, the earliest of the year—
And the wild cypress wave in tender gloom—

II.

And oft by yon blue gushing stream
   Shall Sorrow lean her drooping head,
And feed deep thought with many a dream,
   And lingering pause, and lightly tread,—
Fond wretch! as if her step disturb'd the dead—

II.

Away—we know that tears are vain,
   That death nor heeds nor hears distress—
Will this unteach us to complain?
   Or make one mourner weep the less?
And thou—who tell'st me to forget,
Thy looks are wan—thine eyes are wet.

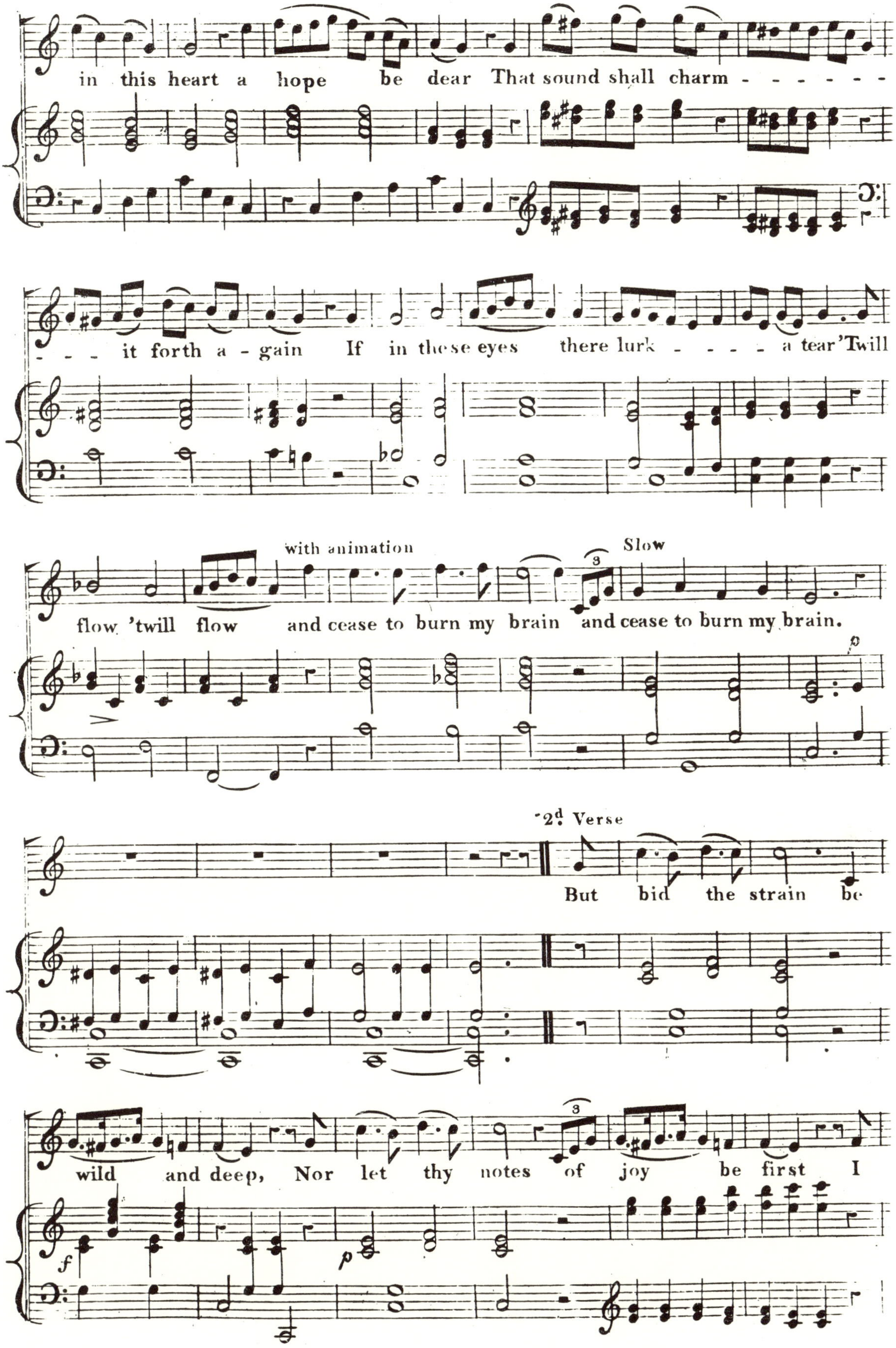
in this heart a hope be dear That sound shall charm - - - - - -
- - - it forth a - gain If in these eyes there lurk - - - - a tear 'Twill
with animation
Slow
flow 'twill flow and cease to burn my brain and cease to burn my brain.
2d. Verse
But bid the strain be
wild and deep, Nor let thy notes of joy be first I

MY SOUL IS DARK.

I.

MY soul is dark—Oh! quickly string
    The harp I yet can brook to hear;
And let thy gentle fingers fling
    Its melting murmurs o'er mine ear.—
If in this heart a hope be dear,
    That sound shall charm it forth again—
If in these eyes there lurk a tear
    'Twill flow—and cease to burn my brain—

II.

But bid the strain be wild and deep,
    Nor let thy notes of joy be first—
I tell thee—Minstrel! I must weep,
    Or else this heavy heart will burst—
For it hath been by sorrow nurst,
    And ached in sleepless silence long—
And now 'tis doom'd to know the worst
    And break at once—or yield to song.

I SAW THEE WEEP.

I.

I SAW thee weep—the big bright tear
　　Came o'er that eye of blue;
And then methought it did appear
　　A violet dropping dew—
I saw thee smile—the sapphire's blaze
　　Beside thee ceased to shine;
It could not match the living rays
　　That filled that glance of thine—

II.

As clouds from yonder sun receive
　　A deep and mellow dye,
Which scarce the shade of coming eve
　　Can banish from the sky—
Those smiles unto the moodiest mind
　　Their own pure joy impart;
Their sunshine leaves a glow behind
　　That lightens o'er the heart.

52

"Thy days are done."

Braham & Nathan.

Marcia

days are done, thy fame be-gun, Thy Country's strains — re--cord, The

Hebrew Melodies / 102

Hebrew Melodies / 104

THY DAYS ARE DONE.

I.

THY days are done—thy fame begun—
    Thy country's strains record
The triumphs of her chosen Son—
    The slaughters of his sword—
The deeds he did—the fields he won—
    The freedom he restored!

II.

Though thou art fall'n—while we are free
    Thou shalt not taste of death—
The generous blood that flow'd from thee
    Disdained to sink beneath:
Within our veins its currents be—
    Thy spirit on our breath!

III.

Thy name—our charging hosts along
    Shall be the battle-word—
Thy fall—the theme of choral song
    From virgin voices pour'd,
To weep—would do thy glory wrong—
    Thou shalt not be deplored!

IT IS THE HOUR.

IT is the hour when from the boughs
    The nightingale's high note is heard—
It is the hour—when lovers' vows
    Seem sweet in every whisper'd word—
And gentle winds and waters near
Make music to the lonely ear.
Each flower the dews have lightly wet,
And in the sky the stars are met :
And on the wave is deeper blue,
And on the leaf a browner hue—
And in the Heaven, that clear obscure
So softly dark—and darkly pure,
That follows the decline of day
As twilight melts beneath the moon away.

Hebrew Melodies / 114

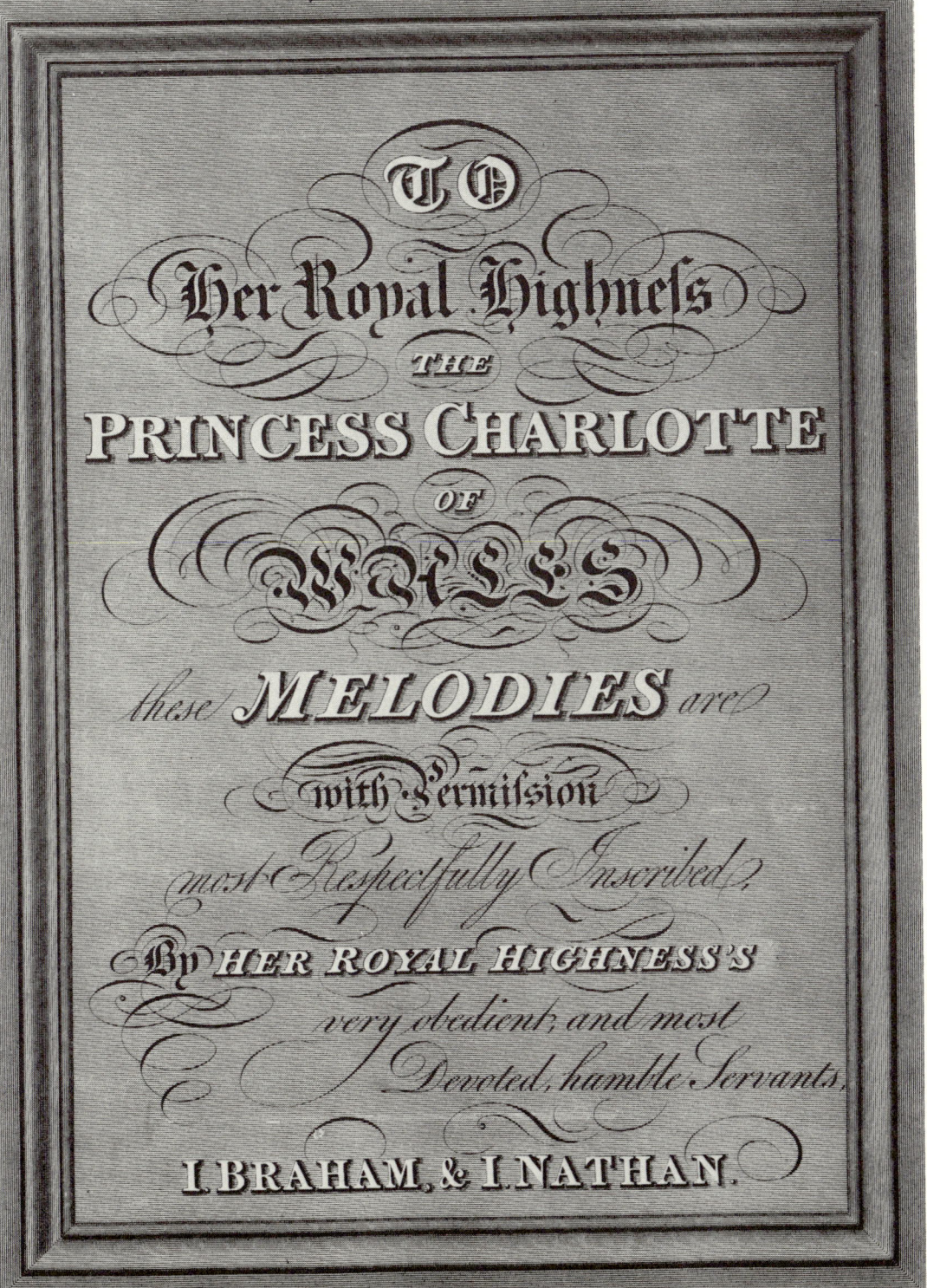

INDEX

TO

THE SECOND NUMBER.

	PAGE.
Warriors and Chiefs!	65
We sate down and wept by the Waters of Babel	71
Vision of Belshazzar	75
Herod's Lament for Mariamne	83
Were my Bosom as false as thou deem'st it to be	86
The Destruction of Semnacherib	91
Thou whose Spell can raise the Dead	97
When Coldness wraps this suffering Clay	107
Fame, Wisdom, Love, and Power were mine	111
From the last Hill that looks on thy once holy Dome	115
Francisca	120
Sun of the Sleepless	129

HARMONISED AIRS,

FOR

TWO AND THREE VOICES.

	PAGE.
We sate down and wept by the Waters of Babel	71
Thou whose Spell can raise the Dead	97
When Coldness wraps this suffering Clay	107
Francisca	123

ERRATUM.

In page 105—first verse, seventh line—for "*the fixed eye,*" read "*his fixed eye.*"

Warriors and Chiefs!

Braham & Nathan.

Martial.

Warriors and Chiefs! should the shaft or the sword Pierce me in leading the host of the Lord Warriors and Chiefs! should the shaft or the sword Pierce me in leading the host of the Lord, Pierce me in leading the host of the Lord.

Expressivo

Heed not the corse, though a King's in your path: Bury your steel in the bosoms of Gath!

WARRIORS AND CHIEFS.

Song of SAUL *before his last Battle.*

I.

WARRIORS and Chiefs! should the shaft or the sword
Pierce me in leading the host of the Lord,
Heed not the corse, though a king's, in your path:
Bury your steel in the bosoms of Gath!

II.

Thou who art bearing my buckler and bow,
Should the soldiers of Saul look away from the foe,
Stretch me that moment in blood at thy feet!
Mine be the doom which they dared not to meet.

III.

Farewell to others, but never we part,
Heir to my royalty, son of my heart!
Bright is the diadem, boundless the sway,
Or kingly the death, which awaits us to-day!

WE SATE DOWN AND WEPT BY THE WATERS OF BABEL

" By the Rivers of Babylon we sate down and wept."

I.

WE sate down and wept by the waters
  Of Babel, and thought of the day
When our foe, in the hue of his slaughters,
  Made Salem's high places his prey;
And ye, oh her desolate daughters!
  Were scattered all weeping away.

II.

While sadly we gazed on the river
  Which roll'd on in freedom below,
They demanded the song; but, oh never
  That triumph the stranger shall know!
May this right hand be withered for ever,
  Ere it string our high harp for the foe!

III.

On the willow that harp is suspended,
  Oh Salem! its sound should be free;
And the hour when thy glories were ended
  But left me that token of thee:
And ne'er shall its soft tones be blended
  With the voice of the spoiler by me!

Hebrew Melodies / 127

Hebrew Melodies / 129

74

Hebrew Melodies / 130

Hebrew Melodies / 132

VISION OF BELSHAZZAR.

I.

The King was on his throne,
    The Satraps throng'd the hall;
A thousand bright lamps shone
    O'er that high festival.
A thousand cups of gold,
    In Judah deem'd divine—
Jehovah's vessels hold
    The godless Heathen's wine!
In that same hour and hall,
    The fingers of a hand
Came forth against the wall,
    And wrote as if on sand:
The fingers of a man;—
    A solitary hand
Along the letters ran,
    And traced them like a wand.

II.

The monarch saw, and shook,
    And bade no more rejoice;
All bloodless wax'd his look,
    And tremulous his voice.
" Let the men of lore appear,
    "The wisest of the earth,
" And expound the words of fear.
    " Which mar our royal mirth."
Chaldea's seers are good,
    But here they have no skill;
And the unknown letters stood
    Untold and awful still.
And Babel's men of age
    Are wise and deep in lore;
But now they were not sage,
    They saw—but knew no more.

III.

A captive in the land,
    A stranger and a youth,
He heard the king's command,
    He saw that writing's truth.
The lamps around were bright,
    The prophecy in view;
He read it on that night,—
    The morrow proved it true.
" Belshazzar's grave is made,
    " His kingdom pass'd away,
" He in the balance weighed,
    " Is light and worthless clay.
" The shroud, his robe of state,
    " His canopy, the stone;
" The Mede is at his gate!
    " The Persian on his throne!"

HEROD'S LAMENT FOR MARIAMNE.

I.

OH, Mariamne! now for thee
   The heart for which thou bled'st is bleeding;
Revenge is lost in agony,
   And wild remorse to rage succeeding.
Oh, Mariamne! where art thou?
   Thou canst not hear my bitter pleading:
Ah, could'st thou—thou would'st pardon now,
   Though heaven were to my prayer unheeding.

II.

And is she dead?—and did they dare
   Obey my phrensy's jealous raving?
My wrath but doom'd my own despair:
   The sword that smote her's o'er me waving.—
But thou art cold, my murdered love!
   And this dark heart is vainly craving
For her who soars alone above,
   And leaves my soul unworthy saving.

III.

She's gone, who shared my diadem;
   She sunk, with her my joys entombing:
I swept that flower from Judah's stem
   Whose leaves for me alone were blooming.
And mine's the guilt, and mine the hell,
   This bosom's desolation dooming;
And I have earn'd those tortures well,
   Which unconsumed are still consuming!

WERE MY BOSOM AS FALSE AS THOU DEEM'ST IT TO BE.

I.

WERE my bosom as false as thou deem'st it to be,
I need not have wandered from far Galilee;
It was but abjuring my creed to efface
The curse which, thou say'st, is the crime of my race.

II.

If the bad never triumph, then God is with thee!
If the slave only sin, thou art spotless and free!
If the Exile on earth is an Outcast on high,
Live on in thy faith, but in mine I will die.

III.

I have lost for that faith more than thou canst bestow,
As the God who permits thee to prosper doth know;
In his hand is my heart and my hope—and in thine
The land and the life which for him I resign.

THE DESTRUCTION OF SEMNACHERIB.

I.

THE Assyrian came down like the wolf on the fold,
And his cohorts were gleaming in purple and gold;
And the sheen of their spears was like stars on the sea,
When the blue waves roll nightly on deep Galilee.
Like the leaves of the forest when Summer is green,
That host with their banners at sunset were seen:
Like the leaves of the forest when Autumn hath blown,
That host on the morrow lay withered and strown.

II.

For the Angel of Death spread his wings on the blast,
And breathed in the face of the foe as he pass'd,
And the eyes of the sleepers wax'd deadly and chill,
And their hearts but once heaved, and for ever grew still!
And there lay the steed with his nostril all wide,
But through it there roll'd not the breath of his pride:
And the foam of his gasping lay white on the turf,
And cold as the spray of the rock-beating surf.

III.

And there lay the rider distorted and pale,
With the dew on his brow, and the rust on his mail:
And the tents were all silent, the banners alone,
The lances unlifted, the trumpet unblown.
And the windows of Ashur are loud in their wail,
And the idols are broke in the temple of Baal;
And the might of the Gentile, unsmote by the sword,
Hath melted like snow in the glance of the Lord!

Hebrew Melodies / 155

THOU WHOSE SPELL CAN RAISE THE DEAD.

SAUL.

I.

THOU whose spell can raise the dead,
  Bid the prophet's form appear.
" Samuel, raise thy buried head!
  " King, behold the phantom seer!"
Earth yawn'd; he stood the centre of a cloud:
Light changed its hue, retiring from his shroud.
Death stood all glassy in the fixed eye:
His hand was withered, and his veins were dry;
His foot, in bony whiteness, glittered there,
Shrunken, and sinewless, and ghastly bare:
From lips that moved not and unbreathing frame,
Like cavern'd winds the hollow accents came.
Saul saw, and fell to earth, as falls the oak,
At once, and blasted by the thunder-stroke.

II.

" Why is my sleep disquieted?
" Who is he that calls the dead?
" Is it thou, Oh King? Behold
" Bloodless are these limbs, and cold:
" Such are mine; and such shall be
" Thine, to-morrow, when with me:
" Ere the coming day is done,
" Such shalt thou be, such thy son.
" Fare thee well, but for a day;
" Then we mix our mouldering clay.
" Thou, thy race, lie pale and low,
" Pierced by shafts of many a bow;
" And the falchion by thy side,
" To thy heart, thy hand shall guide:
" Crownless, breathless, headless fall,
" Son and sire, the house of Saul!"

WHEN COLDNESS WRAPS THIS SUFFERING CLAY.

I.

WHEN coldness wraps this suffering clay,
   Ah, whither strays the immortal mind?
It cannot die, it cannot stay,
   But leaves its darken'd dust behind.
Then, unembodied, doth it trace
   By steps each planet's heavenly way?
Or fill at once the realms of space,
   A thing of eyes that all survey?

II.

Eternal, boundless, undecay'd,
   A thought unseen, but seeing all,
All, all in earth, or skies display'd,
   Shall it survey, shall it recal:
Each fainter trace that memory holds
   So darkly of departed years,
In one broad glance the soul beholds,
   And all, that was, at once appears.

III.

Before Creation peopled earth,
   Its eye shall roll through chaos back;
And where the furthest heaven had birth,
   The spirit trace its rising track.
And where the future mars or makes,
   Its glance dilate o'er all to be,
While sun is quench'd or system breaks,
   Fix'd in its own eternity.

IV.

Above or Love, Hope, Hate, or Fear,
   It lives all passionless and pure:
An age shall fleet like earthly year;
   Its years as moments shall endure.
Away, away, without a wing,
   O'er all, through all, its thoughts shall fly;
A nameless and eternal thing,
   Forgetting what it was to die.

Hebrew Melodies / 164

Hebrew Melodies / 168

FAME, WISDOM, LOVE, AND POWER WERE MINE.

"All is Vanity, saith the Preacher."

I.

FAME, wisdom, love, and power were mine,
   And health and youth possess'd me;
My goblets blush'd from every vine,
   And lovely forms caress'd me;
I sunn'd my heart in beauty's eyes,
   And felt my soul grow tender;
All earth can give, or mortal prize,
   Was mine of regal splendour.

II.

I strive to number o'er what days
   Remembrance can discover,
Which all that life or earth displays
   Would lure me to live over.
There rose no day, there roll'd no hour
   Of pleasure unembittered;
And not a trapping deck'd my power
   That gall'd not while it glittered.

III.

The serpent of the field, by art
   And spells, is won from harming;
But that which coils around the heart,
   Oh! who hath power of charming?
It will not list to wisdom's lore,
   Nor music's voice can lure it;
But there it stings for evermore
   The soul that must endure it.

FROM THE LAST HILL THAT LOOKS ON THY ONCE HOLY DOME.

On the Day of the Destruction of Jerusalem by Titus.

I.

FROM the last hill that looks on thy once holy dome
I beheld thee, Oh SION! when rendered to Rome:
'Twas thy last sun went down, and the flames of thy fall
Flash'd back on the last glance I gave to thy wall.

II.

I look'd for thy temple, I look'd for my home,
And forgot for a moment my bondage to come;
I beheld but the death-fire that fed on thy fane,
And the fast-fettered hands that made vengeance in vain.

III.

On many an eve, the high spot whence I gazed
Had reflected the last beam of day as it blazed;
While I stood on the height, and beheld the decline
Of the rays from the mountain that shone on thy shrine.

IV.

And now on that mountain I stood on that day,
But I marked not the twilight beam melting away;
Oh! would that the lightning had glared in its stead,
And the thunderbolt burst on the conqueror's head!

V.

But the Gods of the Pagan shall never profane
The shrine where Jehovah disdain'd not to reign;
And scattered and scorn'd as thy people may be,
Our worship, oh Father! is only for thee.

Francisca

Braham & Nathan.

Pastorale

Fran—cis—ca walks in the shadow of night, But it is not to gaze on the heavenly light, But if she sits in her Garden Bower, 'Tis not for the sake of its blowing Flower; She listens, but not for the Nigh———tin—gale, Tho' her

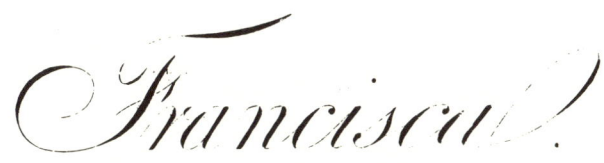

Francisca!

Arranged for two Voices. *Nathan.*

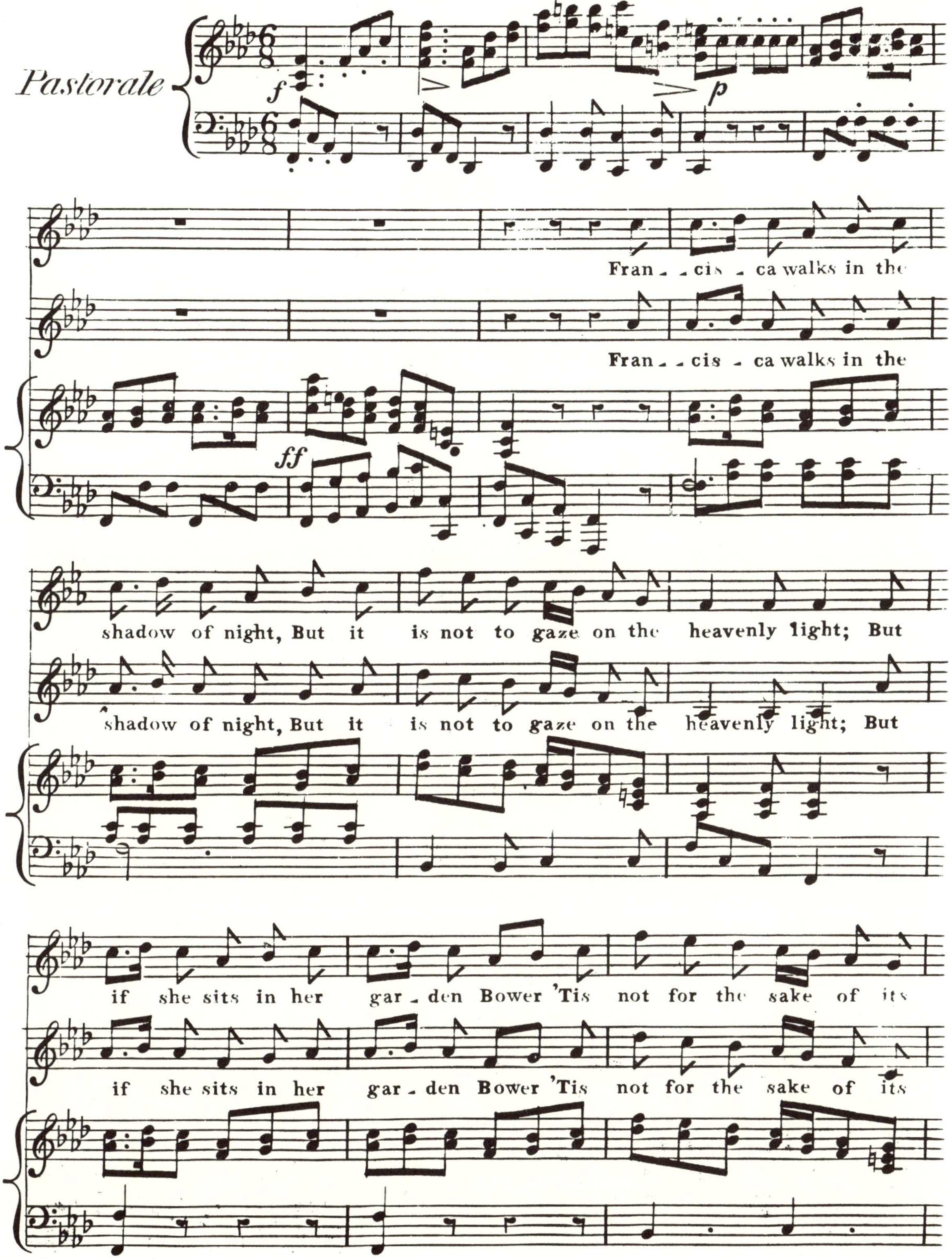
Pastorale
f
p
ff
Fran - cis - ca walks in the
Fran - cis - ca walks in the
shadow of night, But it is not to gaze on the heavenly light; But
shadow of night, But it is not to gaze on the heavenly light; But
if she sits in her gar - den Bower 'Tis not for the sake of its
if she sits in her gar - den Bower 'Tis not for the sake of its

124

Hebrew Melodies / 180

126

Hebrew Melodies / 182

FRANCISCA.

FRANCISCA walks in the shadow of night,

But it is not to gaze on the heavenly light—

But if she sits in her garden bower,

'Tis not for the sake of its blowing flower.

She listens—but not for the nightingale,

Though her ear expects as soft a tale.

There winds a step through the foliage thick,

And her cheek grows pale—and her heart beats quick.

There whispers a voice thro' the rustling leaves,

And her blush returns—and her bosom heaves;

A moment more—and they shall meet—

'Tis past—her Lover's at her feet.

SUN OF THE SLEEPLESS!

SUN of the sleepless! melancholy star!
Whose tearful beam glows tremulously far,
That show'st the darkness thou canst not dispel,
How like art thou to joy remembered well!
So gleams the past, the light of other days,
Which shines, but warms not with its powerless rays;
A night-beam Sorrow watcheth to behold,
Distinct, but distant—clear—but, oh how cold!

Additional Songs

Hebrew Melodies / 194

I SPEAK NOT — I TRACE NOT — I BREATHE NOT.

I speak not—I trace not—I breathe not thy name,
There is grief in the sound—there were guilt in the fame;
But the tear which now burns on my cheek may impart
The deep thought that dwells in that silence of heart.

Too brief for our passion, too long for our peace,
Were those hours, can their joy or their bitterness cease?
We repent—we abjure—we will break from our chain;
We must part—we must fly to—unite it again.

Oh! thine be the gladness and mine be the guilt.
Forgive me adored one—forsake if thou wilt;
But the heart which I bear shall expire undebased,
And man shall not break it—whatever thou may'st,

And stern to the haughty, but humble to thee,
My soul in its bitterest blackness shall be;
And our days seem as swift—and our moments more sweet
With thee by my side—than the world at our feet.

One sigh of thy sorrow—one look of thy love
Shall turn me or fix, shall reward or reprove;
And the heartless may wonder at all we resign,
Thy lip shall reply not to them—but to mine.

Many of the best poetical pieces of Lord Byron, having the least amatory feeling, have been strangely distorted by his calumniators, as if applicable to the lamented circumstances of his latter life.

The foregoing verses were written more than two years previously to his marriage; and, to show how averse his Lordship was from touching in the most distant manner upon the *theme* which might be deemed to have a personal allusion, he requested me, the morning before he last left London, either to suppress the verses entirely, or to be careful in putting the date when they were originally written.

At the close of his Lordship's injunction Mr. Leigh Hunt was announced, to whom I was for the first time introduced, and at his request I sang "O Marimane" and this Melody, both of which he was pleased to eulogize: but his Lordship again observed, "Notwithstanding my own partiality to the air, and the encomiums of an excellent judge, yet I must adhere to my former injunction."

Observing his Lordship's anxiety, and fully appreciating the noble feeling by which that anxiety was augmented, I acquiesced, in signifying my willingness to withhold the Melody altogether from the public rather than submit him to any uneasiness. "No, Nathan," ejaculated his Lordship; "I am too great an admirer of your music to suffer a single *phrase** of it to be lost; I insist that you publish the Melody, but by attaching to it the date it will answer every purpose, and it will prevent my lying under greater obligations than are absolutely necessary for the *liberal encomiums* of my *friends*."

* A *phrase* is a short melody that expresses a musical sentence; a member of a strain or portion of an air. A phrase is in composition what a foot is in poetry, or like the effect of a comma in punctuation.—See Nathan's Musurgia Vocalis, page 99.

Hebrew Melodies, Nº 4.   (105)   Nathan.

Hebrew Melodies / 207

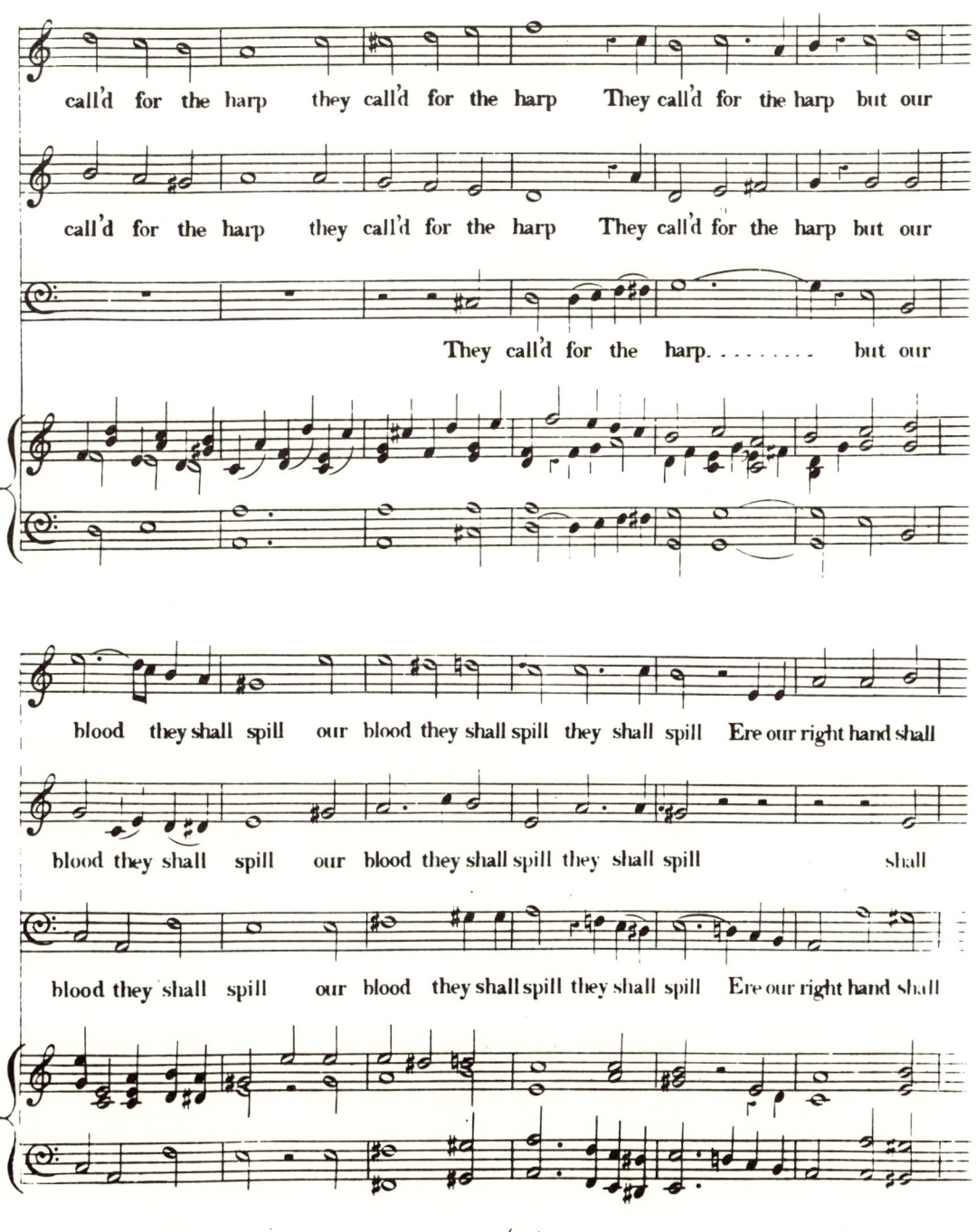

Hebrew Melodies, No 4.   (105)   Nathan.

IN THE VALLEY OF WATERS.

In the valley of waters we wept o'er the day
When the host of the stranger made Salem his prey,
And our heads on our bosoms all droopingly lay,
And our hearts were so full of the land far away.
The song they demanded in vain—it lay still
In our souls as the wind that hath died on the hill;
They call'd for the harp—but our blood they shall spill
Ere our right hand shall teach them one tone of our skill.
All stringlessly hung on the willow's sad tree,
As dead as her dead leaf those mute harps must be;
Our hands may be fetter'd—our tears still are free,
For our God and our glory—and, Sion!—Oh, thee.

The stranger in any country must be impressed with fresh ideas arising from the survey of fresh objects; when those are of a pleasing nature the result must accord in the sequel.

The high places of Salem are here laid waste by the devastating hand of the barbarian, and the legitimate possessors of the country are driven to a foreign land; but, far from being elevated by the change, their joy is turned into mourning: they looked with sorrow on the rivers of Babylon, and gave vent to their feelings in a torrent of tears. The harp is suspended on the willow-tree as useless in this new sphere of existence, and, considering the very use of the instrument, a profanation in the land of strangers, still remembering Sion.

The antiquity of music is beautifully depicted by David in many passages, but in the foregoing lines Lord Byron seems thoroughly to appreciate their force of feeling: as a proof how much he valued this passage of Scripture, it will be observed that two Melodies were written by his Lordship on the same subject, very different in words, but equally beautiful, and will serve as a sufficient apology for harmonizing both.

That it was a theme on which his Lordship pondered with great pathos is also finely illustrated in the following lines:—

"So Juan wept as wept the captive Jews
By Babel's waters—still remembering Sion."

When I submitted the MS. composition of this Melody to Lord Byron he seemed surprised, and observed that the subject had already been published. I pointed out the difference of style in my arrangement of them, and likewise how his Lordship had varied the present version. He remarked that, in writing two, he only wished me to make a selection; "but," added he, "I must confess I give a preference to the latter; and, since your music differs so widely from the former, I see no reason why it should not also make its public appearance."

Hebrew Melodies, No. 4.   (105)   Nathan.

SUN OF THE SLEEPLESS.

Sun of the sleepless! melancholy star!
Whose tearful beam glows tremulously far,
That show'st the darkness thou canst not dispel,
How like art thou to joy remember'd well!
So gleams the past, the light of other days,
Which shines, but warms not with its powerless rays;
A night-beam Sorrow watcheth to behold,
Distinct, but distant—clear—but, oh, how cold!

As a moralist, Lord Byron often calls in the works of nature, and the more sublime parts of the universe, as a proof of the Supreme Being; the harmony of the solar system, the sun, moon, and stars, are duly appreciated, as secondary to their original cause: who can read those sublime lines, and for a moment conceive that his Lordship was the least atheistical in his opinions of things? but, on the contrary, entertained the most exalted feelings and the most sublime ideas in all matters of theology.

In a conversation with Lord Byron, I mentioned to him that several admirers of his writings were sceptical in their judgment as to what his Lordship addressed in this Melody—whether the *moon* or the *evening star*, both receiving their light from the *sun*; to which his Lordship replied, "I see, Nathan, you have been *star*-gazing, and are now in the *clouds*; I shall therefore leave the *Astronomer Royal* to direct you in that matter."

Hebrew Melodies, N.º 4.   (105)   Nathan.

A SPIRIT PASS'D BEFORE ME.

From Job.

A SPIRIT pass'd before me: I beheld
The face of immortality unveil'd.
Deep sleep came down on every eye save mine,
And there it stood,—all formless—but divine:
Along my bones the creeping flesh did quake;
And, as my damp hair stiffen'd, thus it spake.

"Is man more just than God? Is man more pure
Than He who deems even Seraphs insecure?
Creatures of clay—vain dwellers in the dust!
The moth survives you, and are ye more just?
Things of a day! you wither ere the night,
Heedless and blind to Wisdom's wasted light!"

The force of sublimity shown by Lord Byron, when touching upon striking passages of Holy Writ, is particularly fine. The wisdom of Solomon, and the severe trial of Jephtha, are treated by his Lordship with feeling and effect not to be equalled by any other poet; and his admiration of the patient submission of Job is no less forcible in expression and tone.

Being consulted as to his opinion of the authenticity of the Book of Job, he made several evasive replies. I, however, pressed the subject; when he exclaimed, "Nathan, I plainly perceive you are desirous of putting *my* patience to the test." He at length quaintly observed, "The Book contains an excellent moral lesson; we will therefore not attempt to sap its credit or shake its authenticity;" and, to confirm that his ideas were not grounded upon a superficial view of the subject, sat down, and wrote the foregoing sublime lines.

Hebrew Melodies, No 4. (105) Nathan.

WERE MY BOSOM AS FALSE AS THOU DEEM'ST IT TO BE.

Were my bosom as false as thou deem'st it to be,
I need not have wander'd from far Galilee;
It was but abjuring my creed to efface
The curse which, thou say'st, is the crime of my race.

If the bad never triumph, then God is with thee!
If the slave only sin, thou art spotless and free!
If the Exile on earth is an Outcast on high,
Live on in thy faith, but in mine I will die!

I have lost for that faith more than thou canst bestow,
As the God who permits thee to prosper doth know;
In His hand is my heart and my hope—and in thine
The land and the life which for him I resign.

The firmness of faith set forth in this Melody does credit to the general feelings of Lord Byron, in consequence of the re-altered state of the Jews; a feeling which on many occasions he warmly evinced with many liberal remarks.

His Lordship often observed that, notwithstanding the oppressed state of the Jewish nation, though dispersed in every clime, without a fixed country, yet they remain uncontaminated by the creed of any other nation, and retain their original forms of worship with their primitive laws and bonds of union.

"A fabric," observed his Lordship, "on which the lapse of ages has had no power; and, although many sects have risen to their zenith and gone to decay, yet the primitive faith of this people retains every original feature."

The last lines have a forcible allusion to the losses and inconveniences sustained by that people; and at the same time concentrates all hope of alleviation in the power of that God who at first gave them a place in the scale of human existence.

Hebrew Melodies, N°. 4.　　　(105)　　　Nathan.

THEY SAY THAT HOPE IS HAPPINESS.

Felix qui potuit rerum cognoscere causas."—VIRGIL.

THEY say that Hope is happiness—
    But genuine Love must prize the past;
And mem'ry wakes the thoughts that bless.
    They rose the first—they set the last.
And all that mem'ry loves the most
    Was once our only hope to be:
And all that hope adored and lost
    Hath melted into memory.

Alas! it is delusion all—
    The future cheats us from afar:
Nor can we be what we recal,
    Nor dare we think on what we are.

The modesty of genius always appears in the possessor when real merit is taken in the aggregate, and never was more conspicuous than in the person of Lord Byron.

The foregoing lines were officiously taken up by a person who arrogated to himself some self-importance in criticism, and who made an observation upon their demerits; on which his Lordship quaintly observed, "They were written in haste, and they shall perish in the same manner," and immediately consigned them to the flames. As my music adapted to them, however, did not share the same fate, and having a contrary opinion of anything that might fall from the pen of Lord Byron, I treasured them up, and on a subsequent interview with his Lordship I accused him of having committed suicide in making so valuable a *burnt offering*; to which his Lordship smilingly replied, "The act seems to *inflame* you: come, Nathan, since you are displeased with the *sacrifice*, I give them to you as a *peace offering*,—use them as you may deem proper."

Hebrew Melodies, Nº 4.   Nathan.

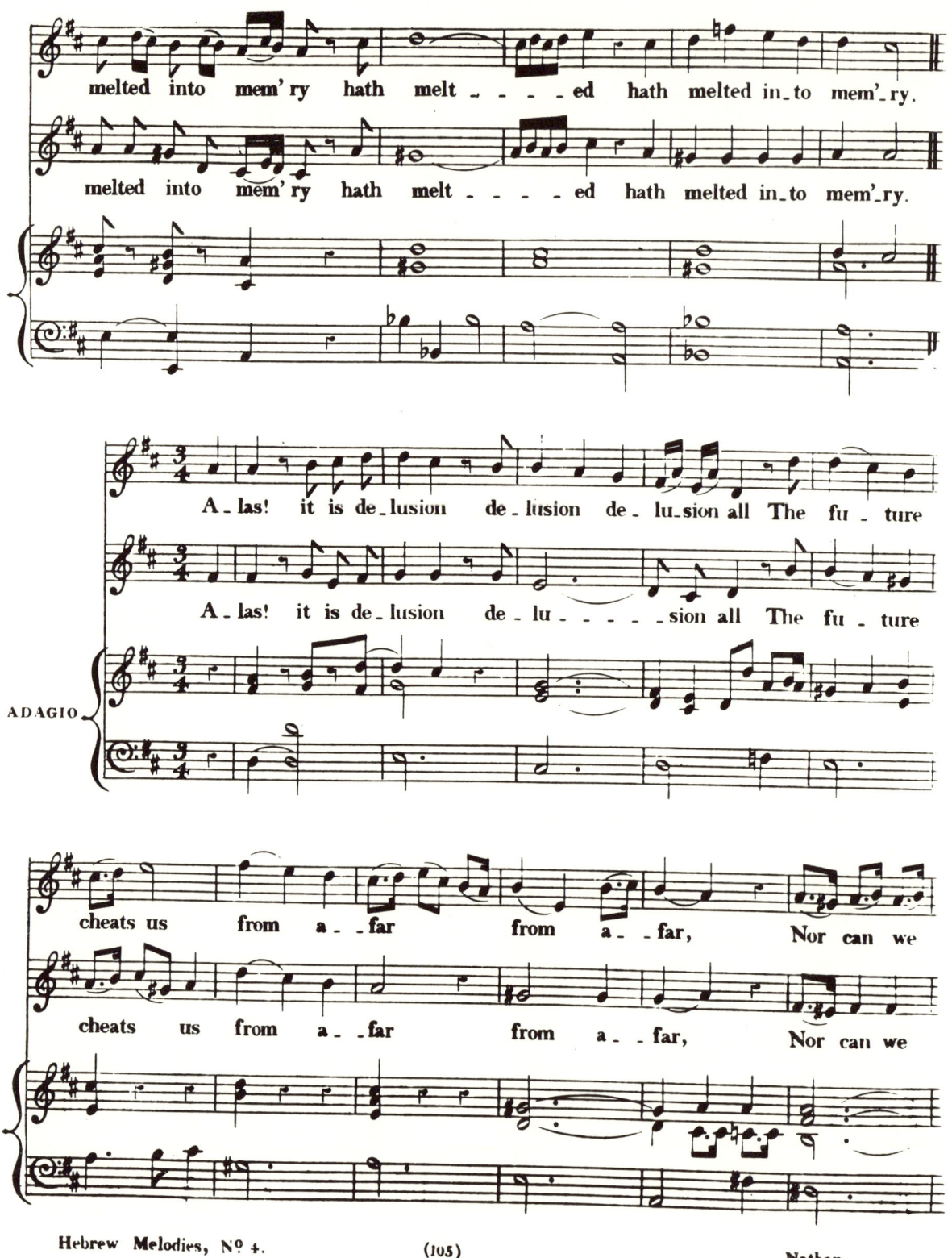

Hebrew Melodies / 239

Notes on the Songs

Songs of 1815–1816 Edition

1. **She Walks in Beauty.** A former *Lekha dodi* of the London synagogues. The 3/4 time marking was and is common for this text, which has produced many melodies. The 1815 version was combined in a single setting in the 1824–29 edition, employing melody #1 for verse one, melody #2 for verse two, and melody #1 again for verse three. Nathan also published in the later edition a trio in A major.

2. **The Harp the Monarch Minstrel Swept.** An almost literal transcription of the melody for the *piyut Ya'aleh tahunen* (May Our Supplications Rise) from the service for the eve of Yom Kippur. Sulzer and Lewindowski record several uses of similarly patterned tunes for this text. Nathan revised the song fairly extensively for the later edition. He reversed the tenor and soprano parts in the quartet, and reduced rests, fermatas, and ornaments throughout. The song was demoted from its #2 position to #8 in the 1824–29 edition, an indication, perhaps, that Nathan remained dissatisfied with it even after many changes.

3. **If that High World.** Francis Cohen, in his article in the *Jewish Encyclopedia,* has said that this melody was still being sung to the Kaddish after the reading of the law in London synagogues in the early decades of the twentieth century. It is interesting to consider, however, whether other texts might not still have inspired the composer. Idelsohn records a variant of *Yig dal* that bears resemblance to the melody of this song:

Listening only to the tunes is dangerous, and sources are rarely certain. Nathan included a trio in the 1824–29 edition.

4. **The Wild Gazelle.** Cohen identifies this as an English folk song adapted in the mid-eighteenth century for the singing of *Yig dal* in London's Great Synagogue. This melody, however, would be difficult to sing to *Yig dal,* a text sung at close of evening service on the Feast of Tabernacles. The first four notes suggest *Bar'chu,* sung for the Rosh Hashanah evening service. And the characteristic figure of the piece, the lilting dotted eighth and sixteenth notes, can be found in several melodies for Rosh Hashanah recorded in Aguilar's *Sephardi Melodies*—for example, the Kedushah for Rosh Hashanah and Ki-pur (p. 28). Note that on page 21 there is an error in the fourth staff, bar 1: the second B natural should be a B flat. The 1824–29 edition includes a harmonization for four voices.

5. **Oh! Weep for Those.** Nathan also added a quartet for this composition, which combines an old blessing chant with what Cohen has identified as "an old northern folk song." The melody comes from the same source as that for "My Soul is Dark." Its patterns are close to those of the High Holydays, especially those of the famous Kol Nidre.

6. **On Jordan's Banks.** This melody is identified with the text *Ma'oz tzur,* a thirteenth-century hymn of German origin sung at Chanukah. Werner records Franck's transcription (p. 91). He notes that other melodies were sung to the text, though this became the most famous. Idelsohn records a version more completely echoing the one Nathan used:

Martin Luther's chorale, "So weiss ich eins was mich erfreut," uses the same tune:

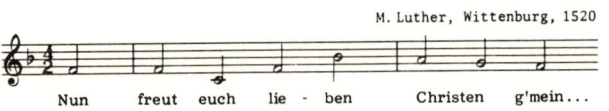

The multivoice setting of this song underwent considerable changes in the later edition, particularly in the tenor and soprano parts. Note that in the solo version of 1815–16 there is an error on the final chord, which ought to have an A flat rather than a C in the bass. The error was corrected in the later edition.

7. **Jephtha's Daughter.** The chant from the Song of Songs, *Shir Hashirim,* still being sung today in the Middle East, bears resemblance to this melody:

In this case, the song's ornamentation increased in the later edition, the effect Nathan sought apparently being a closer resemblance to cantillation:

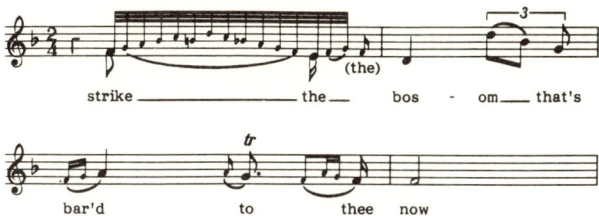

8. **Oh Snatch'd Away in Beauty's Bloom.** The melody bears resemblance to an *Eli tziyan* recorded by Werner, but its origins are uncertain:

The setting is particularly effective in its shift from 6/8 to common time at the conclusion, then its return (in the postlude) to the opening theme, an Italian pattern of composition of solo songs, but one that serves here to remind one of the "pathetic" tone struck in the opening bars. The setting uses three distinct musical motifs to match the three-part elegiac movement of the poetry.

9. **My Soul is Dark.** Another adaptation of the melody of "Oh! Weep for Those." Note on p. 45, fifth staff, bar 1, how Nathan has borrowed a bit of the lilt from "The Wild Gazelle" to daub the line "But bid the strain be wild and deep," an effect he used even more liberally in the 1824–29 version.

10. **I saw thee Weep.** No source known. Nathan made many changes in the later version, manipulating note values to vary the lengths of rests, altering the piano accompaniment, and making the vocal line more rhythmically subtle. Note here a missing accidental on p. 49, staff four, bar 4, where a C sharp has gone unmarked.

11. **Thy Days are done.** The melody's origin is unknown, but it bears resemblance to an older Missinai tune recorded by Werner:

In the later edition Nathan reversed the soprano and tenor parts in the multivoice setting. He simplified by doubling bass and tenor and by restricting the accompaniment. He altered vocal lines enough that the words occasionally fall on notes different from the first version. It is also worth noting that he makes use of an ornament on p. 53, staff five, bar 3 that is reminiscent of ornamentation commonly used in chanting Kol Nidre:

12. **It is the Hour.** No source has been identified for this melody.

13. **Warriors and Chiefs!** Although no specific source has been identified for this song's tune, there are plenty of precedents for the reveille-like melody. Werner records, for example, this Kaddish for the eve of Rosh Hashanah:

14. **We sate down and wept by the Waters of Babel.** This is one of only three duets in *Hebrew Melodies,* including the songs added later. The other two are "Francisca" and "When Coldness wraps." The song has no identified source. In the later edition the piano introduction was altered and the accompaniment's triplets reduced. The lower voice was allowed more initiative. The overall shape of the piece remained intact, however.

15. **The Vision of Belshazzar.** No source has been identified, but the melodic pattern for the lyric's second line ("The satraps throng'd the hall") is typical of improvisational cadences used in cantillation. In the later edition, the key of the setting was changed from C minor to A minor, and Nathan made many minor changes in the vocal line.

16. **Herod's Lament For Mariamne.** This setting has no known source. It underwent the same sort of cosmetic cleanup and rethinking of all the songs before its publication in the later edition. The most effective change was the introduction of some piano triplets in the song's center.

17. **Were my Bosom as false.** No known source. This is the only setting Nathan dropped entirely in the later edition. In the 1829 setting (included in the additional songs), Nathan exchanged cheeriness for gloom, F major for G

minor, 2/4 time for 3/2 time, and conventionality for a degree of peculiarity. Neither version is superior, but the second certainly sets a more obvious, less ironic *tone*. Nathan may have decided that the chromatic cadenzas were too challenging for the audience at which he had aimed—but he did not discuss why he made the change.

18. **The Destruction of Sennacherib.** Source unknown. The early and late versions of this song are virtually identical.

19. **Thou whose Spell Can Raise the Dead** ("Saul" in 1824–29). No sources have been identified for the melodies in this large opera-scena-style piece. The three-voice *allegro maestoso* grew to a five-voice setting in the later edition, necessitating the redistribution of some vocal lines, but the two versions are otherwise interchangeable.

20. **When Coldness wraps this Suffering Clay.** Source unknown. The two-voice setting harmonizes only two of four stanzas—a fact not altered in the later edition, though Nathan made other minor changes in the accompaniment and in the vocal lines, inverting the parts on one occasion. Why the other stanzas were left out remains unclear—in many other cases, he wrote out the music or indicated repetitions in notes for the remaining stanzas of a song.

21. **Fame, Wisdom, Love, and Power were Mine.** Source unknown. The setting did not change in the later edition, except that the accompaniment underwent slight simplification.

22. **From the last Hill that looks on thy once holy Dome.** The source is unknown. Like "Jephtha's Daughter," but unlike the great majority of the settings, this song was revised for greater ornamentation in the later edition. Except for those baubles, however, it is identical in 1824–29.

23. **Francisca.** Source unknown. The later edition changes some harmonies to unisons.

24. **Sun of the Sleepless!** Source unknown. The song was greatly revised in the later edition, and we have included the second version in the Additional Songs for comparison. The melody, changed in many places, still returns regularly to the earlier version. But the new version eliminates all the ornamentation of "glows" and "to joy" in the baroque mode. The difference is emphasized by the less pointedly dramatic prelude and postlude. The later version is perhaps superior because it is less a stylistic imitation.

Additional Songs

1. **Bright be the Place of thy Soul.** First published as sheet music in June 1815, this song continued to be distributed through the following year by the music agent, J. Green (28 Norfolk Street, Strand). Green apparently purchased exclusive rights, for Nathan never reprinted the song nor even listed it in his own catalogue. Note the unusual point that Nathan wrote out several cadenzas for the piece.

2. **I speak not—I trace not—I breathe not thy Name.** Like "It is the Hour," this is a well-crafted piece, intended more for the amateur than for the professional vocalist, yet displaying virtuoso moments in mordants and échappées. We suspect a misprint at the top of page 202, first bar: the E should be an F sharp (compare with all the following versions of this passage).

3. **In the Valley of Waters.** Source unknown. This is a third version of the Psalm 137 theme treated in "We sate down and wept" and "Oh! Weep for Those." Nathan was conscious of repeating the gesture, and he justifies offering yet another version by saying justly that the three songs are unlike (although the setting of "We sate down and wept" shares some features with this song).

4. **Sun of the Sleepless!** (See note No. 24 above.)

5. **A Spirit Pass'd before me.** A challenging piece, this setting might easily have been placed in the first edition, for it was among the early products of the collaboration (October 1814). Yet Nathan saved it for the last volume of 1829. The accompaniment contradicts the view Werner put forth that Nathan wrote only basses for simpletons. Note: An E flat has been left off the key signature on the final page. Source unknown.

6. **Were My Bosom As False.** (See note No. 17 above.)

7. **They say that Hope is Happiness.** A duet showing some of the same inventiveness of "We sate down and wept." This song is definitely not within the range of the amateur. It exhibits an even greater interest than "I speak not" in ornamentation of the vocal line, and like the other duet, "We sate down," it employs triplets. The short 3/4 time conclusion is fascinating, and it introduces a variant of the figure used in "The Wild Gazelle" as a distinguishing motif.

Bibliography

Abrahams, Israel. *Bypaths in Hebraic Bookland.* Philadelphia: Jewish Publication Society of America, 1920.

Aguilar, Emanuel, and D. A. de Sola. *Sephardi Melodies, being the Traditional Liturgical Chants of the Spanish and Portuguese Jews' Congregation, London.* 2 vols. Oxford: Oxford University Press, 1931.

Alderman, Geoffrey. *The Jewish Community in British Politics.* Oxford: Clarendon Press, 1983.

Anonymous. Review of *Hebrew Melodies* (Murray). *Augustan Review,* I (July 1815), 209–215.

———. Review of *Hebrew Melodies* (Murray). *British Critic,* 2nd series, III (June 1815), 602–611.

———. Review of *Hebrew Melodies* (Nathan I). *British Lady's Magazine,* I (May 1815), 358–360.

———. Review of *Hebrew Melodies* (Murray). *Christian Observer,* XIV (August 1815), 542–549.

———. Review of *Hebrew Melodies* (Murray). *Critical Review,* 5th series, II (August 1815), 166–171.

———. Review of *Hebrew Melodies* (Nathan I & II). *Critical Review,* 5th series, III (April 1816), 357–366.

———. Review of *Hebrew Melodies* (Nathan I). *European Magazine,* LXVIII (July 1815), 37.

———. Review of *Hebrew Melodies* (Nathan I). *Gentleman's Magazine,* LXXXV-i (June 1815), 539.

———. Review of *Hebrew Melodies* (Murray). *Gentleman's Magazine,* LXXXV-ii (August 1815), 141.

———. Review of *Hebrew Melodies* (Murray). *Lady's Monthly Museum,* 3rd series, II (September 1815), 169–172.

———. Review of *Hebrew Melodies* (Nathan I). *Theatrical Inquisitor,* VI (May 1815), 377–378.

———. Review of *Hebrew Melodies* (Nathan II), *Theatrical Inquisitor,* VIII (June 1816), 442–444.

———. Review of *Hebrew Melodies* (Murray), *New Universal Magazine,* III (July 1815), 37–38.

Ashton, Thomas L. *Byron's Hebrew Melodies.* Austin: University of Texas Press, 1972.

Bertie, Charles H. *Isaac Nathan: Australia's First Composer.* Sydney: Angus & Robertson, Ltd., 1922.

Beutler, Karl A. *Über Lord Byrons 'Hebrew Melodies'.* Leipzig, 1912.

Braham, John, and William Reeve. *Kais, or, Love in the Deserts, an Opera.* London: Goulding, Phipps, D'Almaine, 1808.

Burwick, Frederick. "Identity and Tradition in the *Hebrew Melodies.*" *Studien zur englischen Romantik,* I (1985), 123–137.

Bush, Geoffrey, and Nicholas Temperley, eds. *English Songs: 1800–1860.* In *Musica Britannica: A National Collection of Songs,* vol. XLIII. London: Stainer and Bell, 1979.

Byron, George Gordon, 6th Bar. *The Complete Poetical Works.* Edited by Jerome J. McGann. 5 vols. Oxford: Clarendon Press, 1980–1986.

———. *Byron's Letters and Journals.* Edited by Leslie A. Marchand. 12 vols. Cambridge, Mass.: Harvard University Press, 1973–1982.

Cohen, Francis L. "Hebrew Melody in the Concert Room." *Transactions of the Jewish Historical Society, England,* II.

———. "Isaac Nathan." *Jewish Encyclopedia.* New York: Funk and Wagnalls, 1925. Vol. IX, p. 179.

Condor, Josiah. Review of *Hebrew Melodies* (Murray). *Eclectic Review,* 2nd series, IV (July 1815), 94–96.

Cooke, Michael G. *The Blind Man Traces the Circle. On the Patterns and Philosophy of Byron's Poetry.* Princeton: Princeton University Press, 1969.

Corri, Domenico. *The Singer's Preceptor: Or, Corri's Treatise on Vocal Music.* 2 vols. London: Chappell and Co., 1810.

Crompton, Louis. *Byron and Greek Love: Homophobia in Nineteenth-Century England.* Berkeley and Los Angeles: University of California Press, 1985.

Dibdin, Edward Rimbault. "Isaac Nathan." *Music and Letters,* XXII (1941), pp. 75–80.

Douglass, Paul. "Isaac Nathan's Settings for *Hebrew Melodies.*" *Studien zur englischen Romantik,* I (1985), 139–151.

———. "*Hebrew Melodies* as Songs: Why we Need a new Edition." *The Byron Journal,* No. 14 (1986), 12–21.

Einstein, Alfred. *Music in the Romantic Era.* New York: W. W. Norton, 1947.

Endelman, Todd M. *The Jews of Georgian England, 1714–1830: Tradition and Change in a Liberal Society.* Philadelphia: Jewish Publication Society of America, 1979.

Evans, Robert Harding. *An Essay on the Music of the Hebrews.* London: John Booth, 1816.

Foreman, Edward, ed. *The Porpora Tradition*. Pro Musica Press, 1968. Masterworks on Singing, Vol. III. Facsimile of Corri's *The Singer's Preceptor* and Nathan's *Musurgia Vocalis*.

Gooch, Bryan, and David Thatcher. *Musical Settings of British Romantic Literature: A Catalogue*. 2 vols. New York: Garland Publishing, 1981.

Hodgson, Francis. Review of *Hebrew Melodies* (Murray). *Monthly Review*, 2nd series, LXXVIII (September 1815), 41–47.

Idelsohn, Abraham Zevi. *Jewish Music in its Historical Development*. New York: Henry Holt and Co., 1929.

Lamb, Charles. "Imperfect Sympathies." In *Works*, edited by Alfred Ainger. 12 vols. Boston: Merrymount Press, 1888, II, 109–121.

Levy, Isaac. *Antologia de Liturgia Judeo-Española*. 2 vols. Jerusalem: Rafael Haim Ha-Cohen, n.d.

Longyear, Rey M. *Nineteenth-Century Romanticism in Music*. Englewood Cliffs, N.J.: Prentice-Hall, 2nd ed. 1973.

Mackerras, Catherine. *The Hebrew Melodist, A Life of Isaac Nathan*. Sydney: Currawong, 1963.

Marchand, Leslie A. *Byron: A Biography*. 3 vols. New York: Knopf, 1957.

Mellers, Wilfrid. *Harmonious: A Study of the Relationship Between English Music, Poetry and Theatre, c. 1600–1900*. London: Dennis Dobson, 1965.

Morel, W. "Zu Byrons Hebrew Melodies." *Anglia*, LXXXIII (1955), 215.

Nathan, Isaac. *A Selection of Hebrew Melodies, Ancient and Modern, with appropriate Symphonies & accompaniments, By I: Braham & I: Nathan, the Poetry written expressly for the work by the Honble Lord Byron*. London: C. Richards, 1815. No. II (also bound together with a reissue of No. I), C. Richards, 1816.

———. *A Selection of Hebrew Melodies, Ancient and Modern, Newly arranged Harmonized corrected and Revised*, Nos. I and II, London: J. Fentum, 1824, reprinted 1827; No. III, London: Mary Ann Fentum, 1828; No. IV, London: H. Faulkner, 1829.

———. "Bright be the place of thy soul" (sheet music). London: J. Green, 1815.

———. *Fugitive Pieces and Reminiscences of Lord Byron: Containing an Entire New Edition of the Hebrew Melodies, With the Addition of Several Never Before Published*. London: Whittaker, Treacher and Co., 1829.

———. *Musurgia Vocalis: An Essay on the History and Theory of Music and the Qualities, Capabilities, and Management of the Human Voice*. London: Whittaker, 1823.

Nickles, Eduard. *Lord Byrons Hebräische Gesänge*. Karlsruhe, 1863.

Phillips, Olga Somech. *Isaac Nathan: Friend of Byron*. London: Minerva, 1940.

Plantinga, Leon. *Romantic Music: A History of Musical Styles in Nineteenth-Century Europe*. New York: W. W. Norton, 1984.

Pönitz, Arthur. *Byron und die Bibel*. Leipzig: Thomas & Hubert, 1906.

Reiman, Donald, ed. *The Romantics Reviewed. Contemporary Reviews of British Romantic Writers*. Part B, 5 vols. New York: Garland, 1972.

Roberts, William. Review of *Hebrew Melodies* (Nathan). *British Review*, VI (August 1815), 200–208.

Sendrey, Alfred. *The Music of the Jews in the Diaspora*. New York: T. Yoseloff, 1970.

Slater, Joseph. "Byron's Hebrew Melodies." *Studies in Philology*, XLIX (1952), 75–94.

Smiles, Samuel. *A Publisher and His Friends, Memoir and Correspondence of the late John Murray*. 2 vols. London: John Murray, 1891.

Weber, William. *Music and the Middle Class: The Social Structure of Concert Life in London, Paris, and Vienna*. New York: Holmes and Meier, 1975.

Werner, Eric. *A Voice Still Heard: The Sacred Songs of the Ashkenazic Jews*. University Park: Pennsylvania State University Press, 1976.

Index

Abrahams, Israel, 11, 31
Ark of the Covenant, 25
Art music of the nineteenth century, 3–4, 30–31
Ashton, Thomas L., 4, 41
Astarte, 26, 30

Bedford Charity case, 4–5
Beethoven, Ludwig van, 12, 17
Blore, Edward, 18
Braham, John, 4, 6, 7, 8, 9, 10, 12, 14, 16, 33, 34, 37 (n. 4, n. 5)
Brahms, Johannes, 30
"Bright be the Place of thy Soul," 8, 23, 24, 27, 28, 29, 31, 32 41, 242
Byron, George Gordon Noel, Lord: collaboration with Nathan, 8–10, 37 (n. 14), 38 (n. 29); and "Byronic Hero," 30; and Sir Peter Parker, 19, 41; attitude to Jews, 6, 8, 15–16, 27; and John Edleston, 27–28, 29. Works: *The Bride of Abydos*, 7, 27; *Cain*, 17, 27, 30; *Childe Harold*, 14, 17, 26; *The Corsair*, 14; *The Giaour*, 27; *Heaven and Earth*, 17; *Lara*, 8, 14, 17, 19; *Manfred*, 14, 17, 26, 27, 30; *Parisina*, 14, 28–29; *The Siege of Corinth*, 21, 28. See also *Hebrew Melodies*

Cantillation, 11–12, 36. See also Synagogues
Charlotte, Princess, 7
Cohen, Francis L., 7, 11, 12, 13, 31, 241
Coleridge, Samuel Taylor, 4, 18, 26
Condor, Josiah, 16, 21
Corri, Domenico, 4, 7, 32, 38 (n. 15)
Curll, Edmund, 15, 16

"The Destruction of Sennacherib," 20, 21, 31–32, 242
Dibdin, Charles, 7, 8
D'Israeli, Isaac, 5

Edleston, John, 27–28, 29
Evans, Robert Harding, 10, 13
Eye: evil eye, 27; power of for Byron, 26–27, 29–30

"Fame, Wisdom, Love and Power were mine," 23, 24, 26, 32, 33–34, 242
"Francisca," 8, 14, 28–29, 35, 36–37, 41, 241, 242
"From the last Hill that looks on thy once holy Dome," 23, 25, 31, 242

Goethe, Johann Wolfgang von, 17
Goldsmid Brothers, 5, 7
Gordon, Lord George, 15–16

Handel, George Frederick, 6, 8, 34, 37; his *Jephthah*, 21
"The Harp the Monarch Minstrel Swept," 13, 15, 23–24, 24–25, 31, 32, 240
Haydn, Joseph, 4, 17
Hebrew Melodies: Nathan's settings of, 30–37; confusion over Braham's role in, 4, 8, 33, 37 (n. 4); copyright dispute over, 9; present edition of, 3–4, 41; performing of, 40; sources for tunes of, 10–14. See also individual songs listed by title
Heine, Heinrich, 3, 14; his *Hebräische Melodien*, 14, 39 (nn. 38, 39)
"Herod's Lament for Mariamne," 8, 23, 25, 30, 32, 33, 241
Hobhouse, John Cam, 3, 9, 10, 16, 18, 24
Hopkins, John, 15, 16
Hunt, Leigh, 8, 10, 28, 30

Idelsohn, Abraham Z., 11, 12, 13, 31
"If that High World," 13, 23, 27, 35, 36, 240
"In the Valley of Waters," 18, 23, 24, 34, 35, 39 (n. 50), 242
"I saw thee Weep," 13, 28, 35, 36, 241
"I speak not—I trace not—I breathe not thy name," 14, 28, 30, 32, 33, 242
"It is the Hour," 8, 13, 14, 28, 32, 33, 241
Ives, Charles, 30

"Jephtha's Daughter," 3, 11, 12, 13, 17, 20, 21–22, 32–33, 241, 242
Jews: Ashkenazic and Sephardic, 12, 31; emancipation of, 4–7, 15–16; political leaders of, 5, 7, 24; stereotypes of, 7, 16. See also Nathan, Isaac: and Jewish image in song

Index / 245

Josephus, Flavius, 17, 25–26; and *Wars of the Jews,* 25; and the story of Mariamne, 25–26

Kaddish, 12, 13, 27, 36, 240, 241
Kenney, James, 7, 8, 14
Kinnaird, Douglas, 8, 9, 10, 14, 18, 23, 24, 26, 28, 37, 39 (n. 50)
Kol Nidre, 36, 240, 241

Lamb, Charles, 6
Lamb, Lady Caroline, 7, 37 (n. 14)
Lassus, Orlandus, 12, 35
Leigh, Augusta, 8, 14, 15
Liszt, Franz, 4, 30
Luther, Martin, 13, 31, 241
Lyon, Solomon, 4

McGann, Jerome J., 4, 22
Mackerras, Catherine, 37 (n. 10)
Ma'oz tzur, 12, 13; and Martin Luther's hymn, 31
Mendelssohn, Felix, 30; his setting of "Sun of the Sleepless!", 34
Mendelssohnian movement, 5, 24
Milbanke, Annabella, 8, 14, 29
Milton, John, 26, 27, 28
Mona, Menehem, 4
Moore, Thomas, 7, 10, 15, 17, 23, 26, 37; *Irish Melodies,* 15, 17, 24; *Sacred Songs,* 17
Mozart, Wolfgang Amadeus, 21
Murray, John, 9, 18, 27, 28, 29, 41
"My Soul is Dark," 11, 13, 17, 26, 32, 34, 240, 241

Nathan, Isaac, 4–7, 37 (n. 10), 38 (n. 29); and collaboration with Byron, 8–10, 37 (n. 14); his veracity, 7, 10; and the Italian style, 30–31, 32–35; and the Jewish image in song, 7, 14, 35–37. Works: *Fugitive Pieces,* 10, 37 (n. 14); *Musurgia Vocalis,* 7, 13, 33, 37; Operettas, 7. See also *Hebrew Melodies*
"National airs," 3, 4, 7, 16, 31, 37

"Oh Snatch'd Away in Beauty's Bloom," 12, 13, 24, 28, 29–30, 35, 36, 241
"Oh! Weep for Those," 8, 11, 13, 14, 16, 23, 24, 35–36, 240, 241, 242
"On Jordan's Banks," 12, 13, 22, 23, 24, 25, 31, 240

Paganini, Niccolò, 4
Palgrave, Sir Francis, 6, 7
Phillips, Olga Somech, 37 (n. 10)
Plantinga, Leon, 7–8
Porpora, Nicolo, 4
Power, James, 7
Purcell, Henry, 8

Quaddish. See Kaddish

Roberts, William, 11, 12, 16, 21, 32, 38 (n. 36)

"Saul." See "Thou Whose Spell can raise the Dead"
Schubert, Franz, 4, 30
Schumann, Robert, 30
Scott, Sir Walter, 8, 10, 18
"She Walks in Beauty," 3, 8, 13, 28, 32, 33, 35, 240
Slater, Joseph, 11, 38 (n. 26)
Smedley, Rev. Edward: his *Jephtha,* 26
"A Spirit Pass'd before me," 22, 32, 34, 35, 41, 242
Star of David: and "Sun of the Sleepless!", 29
Sternhold, Thomas, 15, 16
"Sun of the Sleepless!" 8, 12, 14, 28, 29, 32, 34, 41, 242
Synagogues, 3, 5; Great Synagogue of London, 31; synagogue tunes, 7, 11; synagogue musical practice, 11–12, 31

"They say that Hope is Happiness," 23, 26, 32, 33, 242
"Thou whose Spell can Raise the Dead" (Saul), 17, 18–19, 32, 34–35, 37, 242
"Thy Days are done," 13, 14, 17, 19, 31, 241

Universal Songster, 7, 25

"The Vision of Belshazzar," 14, 22, 35, 36, 41, 241
Voltaire: his *Mariamne,* 25

"Warriors and Chiefs!", 17, 19, 30, 31, 32, 241
"Were my Bosom as false as thou deem'st it to be," 24, 25, 32, 34, 41, 241, 242
Werner, Eric, 11, 13, 241, 242, 243
"We sate down and wept by the Waters of Babel," 23, 35, 241, 242
"When Coldness wraps this Suffering Clay," 23, 24, 26, 30, 32, 241, 242
"The Wild Gazelle," 12, 13, 17, 24, 25, 34, 35, 36, 37, 240, 241, 242
Wilmot, Anne, 14, 28
Worthington, Elizabeth Rosetta, 6, 37 (n. 10)

Zionism, 23–28, 37